"This book is a must read if you see change and disruption coming your way. Read it and keep it as your companion if you are contemplating, preparing for, or experiencing a major change in your life. We are born to manage change and transitions, this book makes it easier to reassemble the pieces of your life and shape the next chapter the way you want it to be."

—Susan Bradley, Founder of Financial Transitionist
Institute (FTI), Founder of Sudden Money Institute

"Financial Literacy is a crucial mission that has had far too little attention and investment. It is near and dear to my heart and I applaud Junko Rivka Horvath for her work in helping women and her dedication to her purpose in writing her book, *Women in Financial Transition*."

—Amy Webber, CEO of Cambridge Investment Research, Inc.

"*Women in Financial Transition* is designed to be read and reread over a woman's life. Changes are inevitable, planned or unplanned, welcome or not. This book is both intensely relatable and authoritative as Ms. Horvath weaves together poignant, real-world stories of women in transition and sound advice from thought leaders in the areas of law, finance, psychology and more."

—Emily Shelton, editor, Financial Services
Directory published in Kiplinger.com

"As an only child, retired teacher, and widow, I could easily have been an "example" in this book. The greatest asset of *Women in Financial Transition* is that it is READABLE, ACCESSIBLE, and NOT written in buzz words and vocabulary known only to those in the business world. A must read for all women!"

—Elaine Drennon Little, author of the novel *A Southern Place*

DIVORCE • INHERITANCE • RETIREMENT • WIDOWHOOD • SALE OF BUSINESS

WOMEN
—IN—
FINANCIAL TRANSITION

SECURE YOUR FUTURE BY AVOIDING THE
MOST COMMON MONEY MISTAKES WOMEN MAKE

EXPERT INTERVIEWS

JUNKO RIVKA HORVATH

Published by Elevate Publishing

ISBN: 978-0-999-19496-6

This book is dedicated to women who are seeking financial security and freedom; women who want to take charge their own finances whether they are married, single, divorced, widowed, or have an inheritance. It is my sincere wish that this book will help you take the first step toward an amazing life of significance and freedom.

ACKNOWLEDGMENTS

TO MY PARENTS, Mutsuji and Ritsuyo Ishigami, who paid for my business school education in the United States, even though they were totally against the idea thirty-two years ago when I lived in Japan. I needed my father to open his wallet. I believe that my M.B.A. degree opened the door for me to survive and succeed in what I do now.

To my husband, Tzvi (Stephen) Horvath for all of his support during the past twenty-one years that I've been in the financial services industry. Without your support and encouragement, I don't know whether or not I would have accomplished what I wanted.

To my daughters, sons-in-law, and my first grandson, Yael and Meir Yaakov Gutman, Adina, Lozzi, and Avraham Tuvia Kosman. You keep my endorphins flowing all day long.

To my clients who trust and let us help secure their financial future. All of your questions and inquiries about your finances have made us more knowledgeable and competent advisors with many ideas in our tool box. Please keep throwing your questions at us.

To the contributors to this book. Without your participation, sharing your stories and wisdom, this book wouldn't have been born. I appreciate each and every one of you.

To my right hand and partner at Fujiyama Wealth Management, Chris Pena, who works tirelessly to find the best solutions for our clients.

To Susan Bradley, founder at Sudden Money Institute, who dedicates her life to coaching us to become better advisors to people in life transitions. I can listen to our clients' inner voices better now because of you.

To my publisher, Cliff Pelloni of Elevate Publishing, who has been helping me write my first book. You are truly a pleasure to work with.

To my spiritual leaders, Rabbi Binyomin and Dena Friedman, who changed my family's lives for generations to come. I don't know how to repay for what you have done to our family.

To my life guides, Rabbi Yechiel and Rebbetzin Miriam Kaufman, in Brooklyn, New York, who have given tremendous support, guidance, and wisdom to me and my family. You are truly a gift from HaShem, which we do not deserve.

Last, but not least, to my friends who are always there to help my family and me. Even my mother, whom I brought from Japan six years ago along with my father who now rests in peace in heaven, feels included within my circle of friends and my community.

CONTENTS

WHAT'S YOUR MONEY STORY?

IT'S HIGHLY LIKELY that you'll experience at least one of life changing events during your life such as:

- Divorce
- Inheritance
- Retirement
- Loss of Spouse
- Sale of Business
- Loss of Parents
- Serious Illness
- Lottery
- Relocation
- Job Loss
- Major Career Change
- Insurance Settlement
- Military Service
- Entertainment or Sports Contracts

How you go through these life changing events depends on *Your Money Story.*

Before we create *Your Money Story,* let's see which side of money you would choose?

There are *Two Sides of Money, Technical and Personal.* Both sides are equally important and complex . . . but *it's the personal side that drives decision-making.*

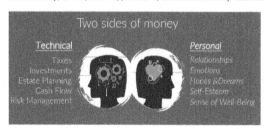

"When money changes life changes, and when life changes money changes." ®
Susan Bradley, CFP®, CeFT®, founder of the Sudden Money Institute

Also, there are *Four Stages of Transition* in life from what was to what will be.

Which stage are you in now?

STAGE ONE: *Anticipation*

STAGE TWO: *Ending*

STAGE THREE: *Passage*

STAGE FOUR: *New Normal*

Four Stages of Transition

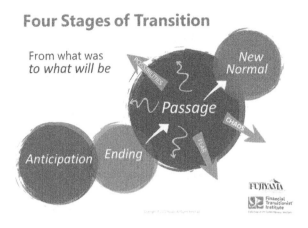

You go through the above stages of transition by *Your Money Story.*

WHAT'S YOUR MONEY STORY?

Your Money Story began before you were in kindergarten, and probably influences your money behaviors, expectations, and decisions to this day.

It was formed by direct and indirect messages you received from your family, relatives, and community. These messages helped formulate how your family talked about money, how they got it, and how they spent it.

Your neighborhood, church, synagogue, peers, and the media also had messages for you about money, whether or not you were aware of it.

All of those messages created your mindset about money when you were a child. And that informed *Your Money Story*, which is literally the narrative you tell about the place of money in your life when you were growing up.

If your relationship with money could use some

improvement, this growth mindset experience will demonstrate that there are actions you can take starting right now, to better that relationship.

You can take a look at where you came from and where you are going, and then assume your position as captain, purposefully steering your powerful boat.

Let's create **Your Money Story** here.

Visit: **www.ChooseYourMoneyStory.com**.

WHY I WROTE THIS BOOK

I GREW UP IN JAPAN, in a traditional Japanese household, where my mother played the docile homemaker and was never involved in business affairs. My father wasn't a controlling type of person, but he gave my mother only an allowance to buy food and necessities for the family. My mother's lack of financial understanding left her vulnerable. I knew that if my father passed away, she would lose his income and any opportunity to maintain the lifestyle she was accustomed to. What bothered me most was that she didn't care. She was happy to live in that sort of "system."

When I was a senior in high school, my teacher visited my parents and me one evening. Soon I would have to choose my future after high school. At that time, it wasn't uncommon for teachers to make house calls a couple times a year to see their students and parents at home. I told my parents and the teacher that I wanted to study business. My teacher told my parents that I should choose English Literature as my college major and become an English teacher because I was a woman. My father strongly disagreed. He believed I should go to a two-year college and become a kindergarten teacher. My mother sort of agreed with my teacher. No one listened to me.

When I went to a college in Tokyo, I majored in English Literature. I was bored. Literature did not excite me. I had wanted my own business since I was a child. I was really good at calculating numbers quickly in my head, and I wanted to use my strengths in my career. When I was a little girl, I used to calculate the revenue of stores near my house. I observed how many customers were entering a store each hour; I guesstimated the spending of each customer and calculated the revenue of the store in my head. Then I would think about ways the store could increase its revenue. My father didn't like when I talked about numbers or what I read in Nikken Newspaper (which is equivalent to WSJ in the U.S.). He said, "Junko, you focus on numbers too much for a girl."

The life my mother was forced to live inspired me to move to the United States and get an education in finance. I wanted to live an independent life with options and opportunities. So, I got an MBA at Georgia Tech in Atlanta. When I began my work as a financial advisor, I assumed that my mother's situation was because of her heritage. However, I was shocked when I quickly realized that many American women, who were educated and had the ability to make choices, also felt stuck like my mother. They too lacked financial confidence, because they let their spouses handle all the financial decisions.

Discovering that this is a situation many women find themselves in regardless of age or culture made me decide that my mission as a financial advisor is to encourage every woman to be more engaged in your household finances. My goal is to be your biggest cheerleader and to work alongside of you, giving you the support and knowledge you need, to confidently have a voice in how to manage your household finances.

This book, *Women in Financial Transition*, is divided by five of life's major transitions: Divorce, Inheritance, Retirement, Widowhood, and Sale of Business. Each chapter begins with two or three real-life stories of women in transition.

Along with my own thoughts, I've added the advice of experts who advise women in need.

If you are expecting one of these transitions in the future, I recommend that you read that chapter first. If your friends or family members are experiencing some of life's transitions, share the knowledge you gain from this book. My hope is that everyone will learn something new that he or she did not know and will avoid future mistakes by learning from my book, not from personal mistakes.

Best wishes for your new beginning!

FOREWORD

By Susan Bradley

I DON'T KNOW YOU. But I know one thing for sure about you: life as you know it today will change, many times. You will still be you, but the way your life works, your routines, patterns, and relationships, will get disrupted. Things will shift, and you will pivot in new directions. Where all that leads is hard to say. With each pivotal event, you will do your best to fully complete the transit from the way life used to be to its next chapter. Everyone does this repeatedly throughout life. You would think that at some point during adulthood, we would become pretty good at these shifts, but mistakes and fumbles are common. Regrets, both large and small, are the norm.

Most of the changes and adjustments we make in life are small; you might not even notice them. Other changes are big events that define new stages of life and the person we become. Culture wants us to prepare for these big events, deal with them efficiently, and get back to normal ASAP. During these pivotal times, efficiency is not usually the best option. Life-changing events call for us to pay attention, be thoughtful and self-aware, and to have patience. The best move is not just survival. These major events are a time to rethink, reboot, and reinvent ourselves—and to move in the direction of our best selves.

Deep within each major life event, welcomed or unwelcomed, is an opportunity to discover more about yourself, find new resources you couldn't see before, and uncover possibilities to create a new version of yourself. It's not always easy; the journey can be tough and even exhausting. During times like these you need a trained thinking partner—someone who understands the stages you are going through. When you feel like you have lost your way, you need someone who understands you to come alongside and remind you of who you are.

Think of this book as a gift. Within this book, you might find your life-transition partner—sometimes the right book is all you need. You might find yourself in the stories. The challenges you face may be named and explained in ways that will ease your concerns and lift you up for the next leg of your transition. The advice Junko gives is universal in many ways, but you will have to personalize it and work with your own financial planner before making big changes.

If you are reading this book as a preparation for a major life change, you might wonder what the big deal is. The events Junko writes about are not uncommon. I invite you to put that judgment aside and read with curiosity. It's not the event that's the big deal, it's the reality of what happens inside people as a result, how those thoughts and feelings affect their lives, and what can be done to minimize the bad and amplify the good. The stories and advice in the book will give you the advantage of a broad perspective of the transitions that follow major life events. This knowledge will help you when it's your turn to navigate the gap between the way life used to be and what comes next.

In that gap, many people feel like they are not themselves; some say they feel like they are in a parallel universe and prefer to get to the other side as quickly as possible. I know that sounds extreme, but once you are in your own big transition you will understand and you'll probably reread this book. Most important, you might be less likely to give up and just "get it over with." Instead, you will be positioned to go the distance. You might be moved to discover, rethink, and transform into the next great version of yourself, rather than rush to get to the new normal people are always raving about and reaching for.

This book is a labor of love and concern written by an extraordinary woman. Enjoy it now and keep it close by; you will want to read it each time life flips and invites you in a new direction.

Susan Bradley, CFP®, CeFT®,
Founder, Sudden Money Institute,
Founder, Financial Transitionist Institute (FTI)

CHAPTER ONE

Divorce

"I feel, whether you're famous or not, transitions are scary for anybody. I feel like change is always scary, but that's only because transition for anyone is new and you wonder how things are going to go."

—NAOMI WATTS, on divorcing Liev Schreiber in 2016, *The Daily Telegraph*

ACCORDING TO THE US NATIONAL LIBRARY OF MEDICINE, National Institutes of Health1[1], numerous studies have shown that the economic cost of divorce falls more heavily on women. After separation, women experience a sharper decline in household income and a greater poverty risk. Their former spouses, in contrast, may even improve their standard of living in post-divorce years. Peterson (1996) quantified the resulting gender gap for the United States, estimating a 27% decline among women and a 10% increase among men in their standard of living. This is a serious issue for women both financially and physically in their own health and in their children's well-being.

To avoid future problems, let's learn from the participants and the experts and professionals in this chapter.

---

1. https://www.ncbi.nlm.nih.gov/pmc/articles/PMC5992251/

AMANDA'S STORY:

Don't Be Blinded by Love

I've been divorced for four years. Throughout my marriage I went through times when I was blinded by love, while other times I was scared to ever leave my husband due to financial reasons. I was financially comfortable.

One day I was looking for something in his backpack and I found a ring that he had purchased. I questioned him about it, and he said that he had bought it for a friend of his because her credit card wasn't working. He said she would be paying him back. I thought it was a little bit strange, but I left it at that. That night, I was watching television. It was close to 1:00 in the morning when he came and told me that he had bought the ring for another woman and that he was leaving me. He went into my girls' room and said goodbye to them. He left us that night. The sad part was that a few months before, we had gone to visit the woman he left us for because he had said that she was sick with cancer. At the time he told me that, just like I had shown kindness to others and visited sick people, he wanted to do the same for his friend. I suggested that we all go together and take a road trip to see her in Florida.

I knew that they had met online through a computer game. I knew this because he asked his mom and me what present he should get her as a group gift since she was having two major surgeries: a double mastectomy and a hysterectomy. We made suggestions like fuzzy slippers and lotions, helping him with ideas, but I always thought of her as just a friend because that's what he told me.

Even though she knew he was married and had met me and my girls, she pursued him and he pursued her. We even took her grocery shopping and out to eat. I was so kind to her. He went back to see her on his own, but again, he said he was just visiting the sick. She even sent us gifts as a thank you for all our help. Little did I know, she and my husband were already romantically involved.

After he left us that night, my husband wanted to come and pack up his stuff. My attorney was very smart and told us not to allow him to do this until he took care of certain things. First, my husband needed to give me a *gett* (a document in Jewish religion that terminates a Jewish marriage.) He also needed to make arrangements to take care of us financially for the next few months. The rabbi who helped me receive the *gett* told me that we needed to catch him while he was there.[2] The next morning, after my husband came to get his stuff, we went to finalize the *gett*. It was a very emotional and difficult time for me; I was extremely sad and I cried.

This all took place in March. A few months later, in August, we had a date for mediation. A friend came with me for emotional support. We sat in one room and my now ex-husband sat with his attorney in another. The mediator spent more time with him because he hadn't come prepared. He couldn't make any decisions! I was so thankful that I had a good attorney who knew what she was doing.

My advice to other women is to keep your eyes open. I was married for nineteen years. Try not to get blinded by love. That's what happened to me. Make sure you know all of your accounts, where all the money is going, insurance policies, IRAs, anything that has to do with finances. For example, I now know he took money out of his IRA to pay for the ring for this woman. At the time, I had no idea how much he had spent on it. A month later, a receipt and the ring's brochure came in the mail. He spent $14,000 on the ring. I asked my attorney to find out how he had $14,000 to spend and found out that it came from the IRA, which was technically both of ours.

Additionally, before remarrying, have a conversation with your spouse about how you will be spending your money together and discuss any big purchases that you

---

2. Rabbi Binyomin Friedman of Congregation Ariel in Atlanta explains. The couple was married in a religious ceremony therefore they required a religious divorce called a Gett to allow for remarriage. As stipulated in the marriage document a divorcee receives a financial settlement however in most cases the civil settlement exceeds the amount stipulated in the marriage contract.

may make. Lastly, it is key to have a good attorney. My ex-husband had a terrible attorney who didn't even prepare properly for mediation, while mine was extremely well prepared.

AUTHOR'S NOTES

Keep your eyes open and don't get blinded by love. Make sure that you know all of your accounts, including your insurance policies, IRAs, etc. Know where all the money is going. It's your responsibility for your own benefit.

TAKA'S STORY:

Find Out Who He Is Before You Get Married

I met my ex-husband in Japan in 1992. He came to Japan through an English teaching program from the United States. We got married in Japan in early 1996 and moved to the U.S. in the summer of that year. I didn't know my new husband's true personality, or that he had a mental illness called Narcissistic Personality Disorder, until after we were married.

I didn't speak English well and I couldn't drive by myself. He drove me wherever I needed to go. It took me five years to become accustomed to living in the U.S. My husband handled all of the family finances. I never had my own individual bank account. Though I had a joint account with him, I didn't know the balances or any transactions—I wasn't even given an ATM card or a checkbook. The max he gave me each time I asked for money was $5 cash. I was never given tax returns to sign either. He told me not to worry about money. Though I wasn't happy, I was afraid of bringing up that topic. Five years after coming to the U.S., my body started to show signs of stress, physically, because I kept everything within myself. I started to have a mouth ulcer, headaches, exhaustion, and social anxiety. Looking back, I must have been depressed. I was a typical hard-working and dedicated Japanese woman. Once I got accustomed to life in the US, I started to work for a Japanese company. I was so busy with my work, cooking and cleaning, and raising two children. I didn't share my situation with anyone since I didn't want people giving me their opinions and judgments. I didn't want to be a complainer, so I didn't call my parents to tell them about the situation either.

One day in 2014 while I was working at my job, I noticed that my phone was suddenly filled with all the messages in "Hangout" app. I didn't even have the app on my phone and I was totally confused. When I opened the app, I saw all the messages that my husband was sending to his girlfriend. The image of my husband that I had in my mind shattered. I became like a dead person. I couldn't put my thoughts together or do anything productive.

He controlled everything—I didn't even have a personal email account. I told my co-worker about my situation and she helped me create my personal email account. I also collected screen shots of all the messages between him and his girlfriend from over the past year on Hangout.

I started going to counseling with a psychiatrist. I had no self-confidence anymore. The counselor said that my husband knew that he could control me and that was why he married me. I simply went along with his plans and put up with the circumstances that he created. I was married to him for twenty years. My counselor said that any western woman would have divorced someone like him much sooner.

Six months after I started counselling, I went to see a divorce lawyer. She charged me $5,000. I borrowed $1,500 from my aunt in Japan and $3,500 from my husband's mother. My divorce lawyer looked at our financials and agreed to help me on a contingent basis. The divorce process took over four and a half years—my ex-husband had been hiding money. The divorce was finalized in 2019.

Through the counselling process, I learned a lot about myself. I learned about transitioning to the next part of my life and the many feelings I would cycle through as I recovered. My counselor showed me a chart of the transition emotions: sadness, self-hatred, anger, sadness, anger, and then healing. I grew up in a culture in which showing my feelings was not a virtue. However, with my counselor I learned that suppressing my true feelings is really bad. My counselor told me to visualize myself at the top of the pole looking down at three train tracks. A train on the right lane brings all my emotions and actions. A train on the middle lane brings all the "why" questions. (Why is this happening to me?) Then a train on the left lane brings my true feelings about what I wanted to happen. For example, the right train brings a memory of me folding laundry by myself. The middle train brings my questions: Why doesn't he help me at all? The left train shows me my true feelings about the situation: I wanted him to help when I asked for help.

This visualization practice helped me keep the panic attacks at bay. The three trains showed me that I live with depression, and that that is okay. For three years, I couldn't go anywhere. I didn't want to take a shower for weeks. I couldn't speak to anyone about it, since I couldn't put my thoughts into words. Whenever I was driving along the highway at high speed, I sometimes had an urge to speed up and be done with life. It was always the thought of my children that stopped my impulse.

This year is the first year since I left my husband that my doctor has reduced my medication. I am happy that I didn't end my life. There are many good things happening. During this period, I have learned that I cannot live by myself and that I should seek advice for things such as money management. If I were my old self, I would have told my financial advisor that I had to do my own research and homework before I would listen to their advice. But now I know that personal finance is not a subject I am good at, and I can delegate it to them with all of my trust.

Now I can notice and appreciate small things such as the blue sky or the beautiful green leaves. I feel so much lighter and it is easier to breathe now. I feel like I am younger, which is a good feeling to me.

Through this experience I learned how important it is to manage my own finances. I will never let anyone control my finances in the future. I also learned to protect myself. I should have done a background check, a personality test, and an STD check on my ex-husband before we got married. I was young and naïve. There were many red flags in our relationship, but youth made me ignore those signs. I tried to see only the positive side of things. I also learned that I shouldn't leave my family, friends—my support group—and my country in order to marry someone, then my stress would have been a half of what I carried.

AUTHOR'S NOTES

Taka's story shows how she went through her transition by facing herself instead of running away from her situation. Her transition is empowering and beautiful. It is like a butterfly coming out of a cocoon and growing wings to fly on her own. She now knows the importance of controlling her own finances and her life. She lives frugally and modestly, and I am sure that her future is bright.

AMY'S STORY:
Don't Lapse Your Educational Credentials

I got married to a physician who did really well for himself. We lived a comfortable life and so I quit working as a critical care nurse. I found that it was necessary for me to stay home and raise our kids: that was a full-time job.

As time progressed, it became obvious that my husband and I were not going to stay together. I decided that I needed to start looking toward the future and began planning what steps I needed to take for divorce. One of those steps was to start my own home-based business so that I would have an income and something to do while the kids were at school. The additional income, alimony and child support would help my fight to keep them in private school and have all of their immediate needs taken care of for several years.

The alimony helped pay for the mortgage, but then the alimony went away and I had to use my savings. I hoped I could keep the house for another year and that I would be able to find additional income to maintain the house. I wanted the kids to stay in the house they grew up in through high school.

Sadly, I didn't think ahead about the kids' college funds. All I got for that was a onetime $10,000 payment. It was a problem that I did not think ahead. My ex-husband was going to give me nothing and he agreed to nothing. A divorce lawyer at least got $10,000 out of him.

In regard to my nursing licenses, I initially did not keep them because I thought, "I'm in heaven and I'm in a marriage." I thought we would live happily ever after and I didn't need to work because he was financially secure. When I knew I was going to get a divorce, I looked into reinstating those licenses. I lost one license because I was late by ten days, believe it or not. However, I was able to reinstate the other license and I have maintained it to this day. Now I substitute and fill in as a nurse here and there. I didn't go back to nursing full-time because there are certain laws in place after all those years of not working. There are still some things that I can do now, but to go into a hospital setting requires a long process.

I spent years raising my kids, which was an important job. If I had to go back through this again, it would have helped if I'd had a checklist of life events to plan for: college, studying abroad, kids' marriages. These are not the kinds of things you're thinking of when you're going through a divorce and you're stressed and fighting. Worst case scenarios with health, death, or other possibilities jump to mind. Wills, life insurance, and things such as changing over the 401(k) were important, but those weren't the only things I should have considered. A checklist would have helped me think of the long-term future.

When you're going through a divorce, you feel like a loser, a failure. Thoughts go through your mind like, "I'm not successful," or "This wasn't what I wanted." Put that aside. There isn't time to mourn right away. You can deal with that later. Get the best advice you can. Take a little piece of this and a little piece of that. Spend the money on an attorney. At first there was a talk of us just going to a mediator, but that would have been beneficial only for him, not for me. The mediator actually took me aside one day, which apparently she is not supposed to do, and told me to "get a lawyer." I took that advice. Women who are going through divorce should think long-term. It's important to have a sounding board around you to help you think through what is happening. Put your emotions and feelings aside as best as you can and just think about your future and all the things that could possibly happen.

AUTHOR'S NOTES

It's a life-shattering experience when a fairy tale story ends and you have to find a way to survive on your own. Amy's story teaches a few valuable lessons to never let your educational credentials expire; you may need them one day. Also, during your divorce, go through a check-list of plans for your future and hire a great divorce lawyer to help you through the process.

One of the best ways to find a divorce attorney who can suit your needs is to find one who has been successful in a case VERY similar to yours. Word of mouth works. Certain lawyers become KNOWN for getting custody for dads (or moms). Others are the go-to for staying with minimal, state set guidelines for child support. Shop around BEFORE, not after.

WISDOM FROM THE EXPERTS AND PROFESSIONALS

Linda Klein, *former President of the American Bar Association, the first woman President of the State Bar of Georgia, and senior managing shareholder at the Baker Donelson law firm.*

After a divorce, I have seen women in particular decide that they're going to start a new life. Unfortunately, they risk the money they have received from the divorce settlement on a business venture. Maybe they open up a little store and they really have no experience in business. Instead of saving the money for their future, they wind up losing it all, and then they really have problems.

My advice to someone going through divorce is this: divorce is stressful enough; don't start a new business venture in which you have no experience. Don't gamble with your future. I realized that that's a strong word to use—gambling—but you really don't need to be gambling with your nest egg. My advice is to start by taking a job somewhere and learn about that business before opening your own. Similarly, don't buy a big house or make very large purchases right away. Take your time and live modestly until you know your long-term financial plan.

This is a similar problem for people who inherit money outright. If you're just inheriting cash outright, making a decision to spend it all is not a good idea. Remember that someone left you that money because they wanted it to be your nest egg.

Alyson Lembeck, *Family Law Attorney and Partner at Ellis Funk, P.C.*

I see a lot of people in crisis. One of the most pressing issues and concerns is the internet and how much it affects marriages. So many problems occur from people creating inappropriate relationships with other people via the internet. Additionally, many people are finding it difficult to communicate within their real-time relationships because of their connectivity to electronics.

One of the financial issues that I'm seeing a lot of is the

lack of understanding in the legal community about the financial needs of a woman who has been out of the workforce for some time to raise her family. (This is true for either gender really, but most often this is true for women.) I think because of the women's movement and the nature of the courts wanting to make sure everyone has equal opportunity to work, it has unfortunately also caused the courts to not want to be as generous, in terms of alimony, to women who have not been working outside the home. I see a lot of judges granting less and less alimony to non-working women who really need the financial help. That is a big concern right now.

I have also seen clients who have a lot of money but who are not good stewards of their money. As a result they face a lot of financial debt that they cannot tackle on their own. This causes them great distress and can really keep them up at night.

In many of my cases there is typically one party who does not have any information about the family finances. This is a common mistake. Many couples trust each other, and therefore one party decides not to be involved in the financial decisions. However, once I am able to work with them, I am able to do what we call in the legal world "discovery," which is asking questions of the other person (the spouse who was taking care of the finances) in order to get all the financial information. This way both parties have an understanding of what's going on financially. Not being aware of that information is a mistake. We are able to overcome that later on by helping couples through this process.

I see a lot of people make financial decisions based on their emotions rather than their financial needs. For example, a woman getting divorced might think she needs to keep the marital home as part of the division, even if she can't really afford it. Usually, if she goes through with it, she won't be able to afford the upkeep of the home, and she'll become cash poor. A good financial advisor would have advised against keeping the home.

One common mistake people make in their divorce settlement is agreeing to divide an asset that cannot be divided, such as certain retirement accounts. It is important to research the best way to divide retirement accounts in advance of finalizing the divorce. I had a client who agreed that she would get half of a retirement account. Yet, after the agreement was signed and she tried to divide the account, she was told that the account was not divisible. There are retirement accounts, such as certain teacher retirement accounts, that are not divisible. Other qualified retirement accounts, such as a 401(k), are divisible. However, the only way to divide the money is to obtain a Qualified Domestic Relations Order (QDRO), which is a specific order that the judge in your case must sign before the funds are divided. If you have a 401(k) that you are dividing, everyone's agreement should specify that they need a QDRO, how the division will be implemented, who will draft it, and who will pay for it. I personally have seen agreements where these details are not specified and that causes problems to arise later.

Another common mistake after a divorce is not checking your beneficiaries. For example, on your life insurance policy, make sure that you have changed your beneficiary to someone other than your ex-spouse. However, if you are ordered in the divorce to keep your ex-spouse as a beneficiary, make sure to do that. The person listed as the beneficiary should require proof every year that they are listed as beneficiary. I had a client who did not do that and, unfortunately, the spouse died without keeping the life insurance benefit in place. This caused a big problem and my client had to fight the life insurance company to receive the death benefit that she was entitled to.

One last common mistake that people make is putting too much sensitive information in their documents. For example, if you are required as part of the divorce to sell your home, there are a lot of details that go into the negotiation. Often, there are certain specifications in selling the house: it must be listed at a certain price, it must be sold if a certain price is offered, and there are specific terms of how the house sale will happen. In my cases, I always include a side agreement that none of that information is put into the public record. People can look up that information and get those documents as part of the public record and then negotiate to try to get your house for less than you are asking because they know you have to sell it at a certain price point per your divorce. One easy way to avoid this is to make it a side agreement that is not filed with the court.

These are just a few mistakes that can be avoided, especially if you have a good attorney to assist you to ensure you are properly protected in these areas throughout your divorce.

Tina Shadix Roddenberry, *Family Law Attorney and Shareholder at Boyd, Collar, Nolen, Tuggle, & Roddenbery, LLC*

The pressing issues, concerns, and problems that divorcing people face depend on whether they have children or not. If they have children, one of the primary concerns is custody, how the children will react to the divorce, and the impact it will have on them going forward. Another primary concern, whether they have children or not, is financial. How they will support themselves? What financial support will they get on a monthly basis to pay their bills? How will they divide their assets? If they are not working, do they now have to get a job?

How will their lifestyle change? Will they have to move out of their house? The breadwinner in the marriage may worry if he or she will have enough left to live on and to retire after paying the spouse and the alimony.

Divorce and the issue of finances are often more stressful for the financially dependent spouse, with the concerns of whether they can stay in the house or afford to pay the bills. If they have children, they often don't want to have their children go through the whole transition of the divorce and then, on top of that, have to move and leave their friends or change schools.

Whether it's a good idea to stay in the house and keep it depends on your financial circumstances and the financial estate. If it's a large estate, yes. But if the estate is really just retirement and equity in the home, then it oftentimes does not make sense to stay in the home. You have to look at the whole picture. For example: if you have children who have special needs, how would a move impact them in adjusting to a new school and forming new relationships with their friends? I often refer my clients to a financial planner and have them look at an estimate of what they might receive in the divorce. We are lawyers and we give people legal advice. We don't give them financial advice; the client has to decide on their own what financial decisions they want to make.

One mistake I see is when couples start discussing their settlement without getting legal advice or knowing what they're entitled to. I have had clients (usually in a situation where one spouse is more dominant and controlling and the other spouse is more submissive), who have been talked into a settlement that is not at all equitable or what the Georgia courts would do. I've been able to come in and give advice, helping my client realize all they are entitled to and to get out of previously made agreements.

Another mistake I see often is if a spouse wants to be involved in parenting their children, but they've already moved out of the house. Not living in the house means they do not have much time with the children. If it's a contested custody case, the judge will look at which parent is there every day caring for the children. In cases like this, I work quickly to get my client back in the home. In this way, they are parenting every day.

I've had situations in which people I did not represent in their divorce come to me with questions and problems. Some of these problems are because they have not thought out the tax consequences of some of their assets and as a result they've made some bad decisions. For example, let's say the marital state is equity in a home of $200,000 and they have a retirement of $200,000 and one says to the other, "You keep the house, and I'll keep the retirement." It looks even on paper. But what they did not take into account was the fact that the retirement had not yet paid taxes. This is all pre-tax money. It's not really $200,000 to the person who receives it; it's $200,000 minus approximately 35%. At that point there's nothing they can do. Once you've divided the assets, you're stuck, and I can't change that. I've also seen cases where a client has agreed that the alimony they pay is non-modifiable. That means that it stays at that level for the whole period of time and doesn't change. Once that decision is made, you can't get out of it. That's a mistake that people make instead of allowing it to be modified.

A tax issue to consider is joint debts in both parties' names when they have not protected themselves to make sure that the debt is paid off. For example, the agreement will say that the husband or wife will pay the debt, even though it is in both of their names. If the husband or wife doesn't pay the debt as promised, it affects the credit score of the other spouse. Some people don't realize that the creditor will still come after them—they don't care what the agreement says. We always try to make sure that any joint debt is paid off or put in one party's name rather than left as a joint debt.

Another mistake that happens is when one party chooses to keep the house. Oftentimes, that spouse will refinance the mortgage. Mortgages are usually a joint debt. Let's say the wife is keeping the house and she needs to refinance it. However, she hasn't checked beforehand to see if she qualifies and what her payments will be. In the end, she's in a bad financial situation, she can't afford the refinancing, and she has to sell the house.

Lastly, I sometimes see people involve their children in their divorce. Whether they share some things the other parent did wrong or talk to them about the divorce details. This is very bad for the children and it causes more conflict than is necessary. These are just a few mistakes to be wary of.

Catherine Sanderson, *Family Law Attorney and Partner at Sanderson & Sanford, LLC*

Generally, the women I see going through divorce fear the unknown. This is the biggest problem. Sometimes I have women who come in who have been married for twenty years and who have never been responsible for their finances. And even if they are financially responsible, they don't know anything about their retirement savings or retirement planning. They come in very frightened about how they are going to move forward, managing their household, paying their current expenses, and what they are going to do for retirement when they reach retirement age. Those are the fears I see the most.

Oftentimes, when I have women clients in long-term marriages, they just don't know what is out there. They don't know what savings or retirement money they have because somebody else has controlled all of that for an extended period of time. They often don't even know how to find out that information.

Most of the time, even in shorter term marriages, men handle the finances. In longer term marriages, marriages of twenty years or so, women are particularly vulnerable because they have gone for a long period of time not managing on their own. This is why folks who had established careers or established lives before they got married are less fearful than those who got married at a young age and never had that control. The one thing that keeps them up at night is how they are going to make it on a monthly basis without that double income or without the breadwinner's income. Even in households where the wife has also been working, her earnings may not be sufficient to live the way that they were living. They might have a larger house than she can afford on her own. I have seen that the house itself is often a big worry. She wonders if she will be able to keep the house or have to sell it, and many times, there's a lot of emotion tied in with the idea of having to lose the house.

In the last five years, I've seen fewer women choosing to keep the house than I did earlier in my practice. Now, if the mom has custody of the children, she often wants to keep the house for them because of the emotional attachment, provided she can afford it. However, keeping the house can be a pitfall for some women because it might not be a good financial decision. Additionally, as things have changed in society and in the courts, it is less likely that the court is going to make it financially possible for the mom to keep the house. In the past, alimony or some other financial settlement would pay the mortgage for a few years. Now it's more common for the court to decide that if the mom can't afford the house on her own, it has to be sold.

It's very important to me to help my clients understand that they don't need to keep the house. I try to help people see the reality of what they can afford so that in the divorce proceedings, what we ask for puts them in a good position for their future, rather than asking for something that ultimately isn't going to work out. I had a client years ago who insisted on keeping an expensive house. She was sure that she could make it work between the retirement, savings, income, alimony, and child support she had been awarded. I tried to get her to give up the house, but she ended up getting it instead of some other assets. For example, let's say there was $500,000 in a 401(k); she could have gotten half of that, but instead, she took more equity in a house that she couldn't afford. She ended up losing it and the house was foreclosed upon. Not only did she lose all of the equity that she would have had in that house, but also the 401(k) that she gave up in order to keep the house.

I personally learned a lot from that situation; I frequently tell people about that case as a warning. A house isn't a bad investment if there's a lot of equity in it, you can manage your monthly payments, and you have a good income source. Then certainly sometimes it makes sense to take the house instead of some other asset. But, it's important not to let your emotional attachment to a house or your belief that your children must have that particular house outweigh good financial decisions when you are looking at the whole package. Children are a lot more resilient than people realize; what makes a house is the parent not the building. Financial stability is so much more important than your home address.

Another thing that people need to think about, even if they have absolutely no intention of getting divorced, is how they handle their separate assets during their marriage. For example, when two parties are married and the wife inherits $100,000, if she puts that inheritance into a joint account it becomes their marital asset. Three years later, at the time of their divorce, if that money has been spent, her inheritance is gone. But let's say that the money has been put into their joint account and used for joint expenses such as the marital home that was in both parties' names. That inheritance money becomes marital property. Now, her inheritance is gone and he gets half of it.

If you or your spouse inherits, it is important that you make sure that you're being fair with where that money goes moving forward, even if you have no inclination toward divorce. Be smart and think about all of the possibilities and protect your assets. I have seen devious people who have separate personal and joint accounts. In their marriage, they spend all of their joint money. The person in charge of the finances secretly keeps their own money separate, but spends all of the joint money. In the end, one person has a couple hundred thousand dollars in inheritance money that was never touched and the other person has nothing.

Another area that people sometimes don't think about during a divorce is getting remarried. Let's say a couple has children when they divorce, but then they remarry. It's really important that when they do remarry, that they have an agreement of what happens financially upon their death. By remarrying, their new spouse becomes the inheritor if they die without a will. Even if they do have a will, the new spouse can take a year of support and their partner's children may lose out on inheritance. I've seen folks struggle after the death of a spouse in a blended marriage, making sure that everybody's interests are taken care of fairly.

Erin Stone, *Family Law Attorney and Partner at Bovis, Kyle, Burch & Medlin, LLC*

One of the most pressing issues I'm seeing lately is people getting divorced later in life, either near or during retirement. These days, people are living longer and healthier to an older age and so they are looking at a longer retirement. Sometimes they realize, when they've retired and everybody stops working and instead spends more time together, that they're not in a happy marriage. They don't want to stay together. What I find is that it's harder for people to think in terms of changing their financial plans at this stage in life. It's harder for them to separate the emotional feeling of ending a very long marriage and looking at the more practical aspects of how that joint retirement plan that was put in place for the two of them can be divided and still give them the financial security that they need.

When they start looking at divorce, oftentimes the wives, who have mostly been the homemaker raising the children, really have a hard time understanding what they have and whether it will be enough to support them into the future. I recently worked with a woman who, in looking at her future plans, really wanted to stay in her home and wanted her husband to continue to support her after the divorce. But because they were both retired, there really wasn't enough income coming into the marriage for the husband to keep her supported through alimony, dividing up their savings, and their retirements. So we had to come up with a plan that would give her what she needed financially, but also leave him enough so that he could move forward financially as well.

When a couple gets divorced, both of their lifestyles are going to change; their needs are going to be different. We have to look at the reality of what is really there. If the husband is still earning high amounts, he can more than afford to pay alimony over time. But if both of the spouses are retired, then we have to look at the pie that is left and divide it between the two of them so that they each will have income generating assets and be able to draw on that retirement in the long term.

In terms of the Social Security, they will each be eligible to get their Social Security after ten years of marriage. If the wife makes the lower income, she will be able to claim half of the husband's Social Security, so she'll have that income as well. But most people make a financial plan assuming that they're still going to be together, sharing their savings in one household. Once you divide it into two households, you're doubling the expenses. Once that divorced spouse remarries, they lose the claim to their ex-spouse's Social Security.

As a trend, I am seeing more divorces in same-sex marriages, mainly because it has only been a few years since this was made legal. Inevitably some of those marriages are going to end in divorce. Some become interesting cases because those couples often do not have a good understanding of what it means to be married from a financial standpoint, since they've only had that status for a short time. Marriage changes the way the finances are handled in a household, as opposed to couples who live together outside of marriage. Same-sex couples who marry are treated like every other married couple at this point and so the marital estate is divided between them. Therefore, any property that they acquired during the marriage, that is not a gift or an inheritance, is divided between the couple when they get divorced. The other thing that has changed is the spouses' right to claim alimony for every child. Just like in every other marriage, usually one spouse is a higher earner than the other and the lower earning spouse needs spousal support or alimony. Over time, this will become more normal to same-sex couples, but for right now, it's a new idea they are getting used to.

One of the mistakes I often see people make is thinking they can hide their bad behavior when they really cannot. For example, I recently represented a wife whose husband was cheating on her. He thought she had no idea because he used a credit card to charge all of his expenses for the girlfriend: hotels, gifts, jewelry, etc. He thought that because those credit card statements never came to their house, she would never find out about them. However, he paid those bills out of his bank accounts. We were able to trace those financial transactions and discovered everything. People sometimes think that they're being very clever, but because we do so many transactions electronically, credit cards, phone payments, PayPal, etc., there are records that create a trail we can follow. It makes it easier to track where people are going and what they are doing.

I represented a woman years ago whose husband would have his girlfriend meet him at different locations when he was traveling for work. He had a business credit card that he would charge those expenses to. During a divorce case, we're able to investigate all of those financial transactions. We ended up finding out what he was doing and helped my client, the wife, recover more of the marital estate to get more alimony.

Be very careful with technology. It is so helpful, and it does make everything in life easy, but sometimes it becomes too easy. I'll give you another example of where technology tipped off a client. Many people have an iCloud account that they share. Oftentimes, they have a family account to share pictures, and sometimes there's also a family email address. When you get divorced, you must separate those accounts. It's hard to remember throughout the process what you share, what you don't, and who has what passwords.

I had a client whose divorce was pending. He forgot that he was sharing an iCloud account with his soon to be ex-wife. Unfortunately, he didn't realize that because they shared the account, she was also receiving all of the text messages he was sending to his girlfriend. His wife was reading all the messages he sent not only to his girlfriend, but to other people like me, his lawyer. He could not, for the longest time, figure out how she knew everything he was doing. We had to sit down with him in our office and think about all of the different accounts and passwords that they might have shared so that he could fix this problem and regain his privacy and confidentiality.

Those kinds of situations happened in several cases before we started sitting down with our clients at the beginning of a case and making sure that they changed all their passwords and separated their online accounts. It can be a problem especially if text messages, emails, and pictures are incriminating in some way. Again, word to the wise, technology makes everything easy, but always be careful about who can see your information and whom you are sharing it with.

Tracy Ann Moore-Grant, *Attorney, Mediator, and Arbitrator, Patterson Moore Butler*

I started the Amicable Divorce Network (ADN) group in June 2019 because I didn't like the way the family law system was designed and I wanted to address the issues I saw my clients facing.

I often had clients, reasonable people, who simply wanted fair, normal results for their divorce case and for it to take a reasonable period of time. They would ask me questions about how long the process would take and how expensive it would be in the end. Without fail, the answer was: "It depends on who your spouse hires." This was a big frustration for me. The destiny of my clients, their litigation costs, stress, and how long the process would take, was almost solely in the hands of another attorney. Their spouse could hire anybody.

There are people who are very driven by litigation; they increase conflict in a case, file things they know are neither necessary nor valid, and they increase litigation costs unnecessarily. I was really frustrated that people with good intentions had to go through terrible divorces because of the other attorney. As a mediator, I have gone into mediations in which the parties were originally on the same page. They sat down at the kitchen table and reached an agreement. However, the wife then took their informal agreement to an attorney and it blew up. The reason for the blow-up was the attorney's financial gain. I wanted to find a way for people to hire attorneys who honored their wishes, who were settlement-minded, reasonable, and who did not have reputations for overbilling or engaging in unnecessary conflict. That was my primary issue with the family law system.

Most of the attorneys involved in the Amicable Divorce Network work at a reduced hourly rate—they are essentially losing money to do it. Yet we have an incredible number of people who have come to this network—top attorneys in every area of Georgia—regardless of their financial gain, because it's the right thing to do. Our network philosophy aligns with the mindset that, as attorneys, we're working for what's best for the client. Sometimes that means extensive litigation—those situations still exist. By creating the network, I'm not saying there aren't cases that don't need judicial intervention. We sometimes have cases involving family violence, mental health issues, and other circumstances that are appropriate for court. However, cases that involve a very standard family law situation often resolve in meditation. For such cases, we have the Amicable Divorce Network.

The Amicable Divorce Network (ADN) was a concept I had last June. I had lunch with a few professionals in my area who felt the same way about the family legal system. At that meeting, they said "Let's get this started." They wrote a check and asked to be involved. That's how I started. It has been a lot of work, but I'm passionate about doing things well.

From my research, companies that promote amicable divorces are uncommon. There may be local organizations or businesses that promote amicable divorce practices, but to my knowledge, there are no state or national organizations in the United States that handle these cases. We are limited by geography; there are only so many people per category per county. In my research, I've found that the Collaborative Law movement is the closest to what we do in ADN. However, they had some issues I did not like. One issue was requiring their clients to use a pod of professionals. In the Collaborative Law movement, each person has an attorney, a financial professional, a mental health professional, and one more person on the team. Most normal income families can't afford five professionals involved in their divorce, even if they're of a collaborative mindset. It's not financially feasible.

In our network, we have the best people available for our clients if they want that resource. They're the best in their industry who meet our requirements: they have been licensed for at least five years, they have had no disciplinary actions, they have been either invited or vetted by the group: not everybody makes it. With Collaborative Law, if you engage these professionals in a divorce and it doesn't result in a settlement and has to go to court, you cannot use any of them in your divorce hearing. There is no confidentiality in the collaborative divorce process. This is not the case with Amicable. Our clients have an attorney who is bound by confidentiality. They have a settlement mindset—they are negotiating on behalf of the client. They're getting the information that is needed for a settlement; they're not gathering all kinds of unnecessary information, and they're not threatening court actions. These are attorneys who look at a holistic approach for families. We call in a parent coordinator and the best mediators for our clients' cases. When I set up ADN, I saw no reason why people should compromise their confidentiality or have to start over with new professionals should the case go to trial. That is financially prohibitive for a standard family.

Emily W. McBurney, Esq. *QDRO attorney at Emily W. McBurney, P.C.*

I've been giving presentations about QDRO to attorneys, divorce lawyers, family law attorneys, and financial professionals for almost twenty years. Most people don't know what a QDRO is or why they would need one. A QDRO is a Qualified Domestic Relations Order. I've had cases over the years in which people came to me and said, "I got divorced 15 years ago and in the divorce I'm supposed to get half of his pension. He just died, or he just retired and I'm waiting for my payments to start, but they haven't started." Often this is because nobody did QDRO or even told them that they needed one.

Oftentimes, in a pension plan when someone dies, there's nothing you can do (there are some exceptions to that). If someone retires, all of the options have been foreclosed. Unless an actual QDRO is done, signed by the judge, and approved by the plan administrator, you will not get your share of the 401(k) or the pension; you don't have anything. The problem is that most people going through a divorce have no way of knowing that.

Not all retirement assets can be divided. I prefer to get involved in a case before the agreement is made so that I can say "no, that's not divisible, don't agree to divide that." But most often people come to me after the divorce is final. That's one of the reasons why I try to educate the divorce lawyers because it's better to find out before making a deal. Sometimes they come to me and I can see right away that they've made a deal to divide a retirement asset that I know is not divisible. There are ways to help: whether to trade off another asset or to have specific wording in the agreement. For example, in the agreement you can add wording that states "the husband has this supplemental executive retirement plan that's not divisible and it can only be paid to him. But when he gets his payments in the future, he must pay X amount to her. (Then they have to deal with the tax issues because those payments will be made taxable to him.) That's the kind of thing people are devastated to find out after the fact. I do a lot of work amending people's divorces because they have agreed to do something that is not doable or the judge has ordered something that is not possible because the account is misidentified. For example, sometimes an account is labelled a 401(k), but it's really an IRA, and that is a different process.

A lot of these circumstances stem from basic ignorance. Because there are so many things on fire in divorces, retirement assets can sort of fall to the wayside and clients don't want to pay to investigate. I get a lot of cases where people come to me and say, "My divorce agreement says I'm going to get half of his teacher's pension by QDRO." I have to tell them that they can't and that there is no power in the world that will let them do that, and we have to redo the agreement. Once the agreement is already signed, gaining the cooperation of the spouse who really isn't interested in paying part of their pension to you is much harder than if it had been handled correctly at the negotiation table.

Several years ago, a man who was an executive at a big company and who had a lot of money, came to me and said, "I need to hire you to do a QDRO. I got divorced 16 years ago and didn't have an attorney because we were just agreeing to everything. I agreed for my wife to get a share of my pension, the QDRO was done, and now I'm about to retire. When I got the estimate of what I'm supposed to receive from my pension, it's about a half a million dollars less than I was expecting."

I looked into his case and said, "Here's the problem. Your agreement says that she is going to get 50% of the value of your pension at the time of your retirement, not at the time of your divorce. You've been working these 16 years, accumulating a lot of pension benefits. She's getting half of that, not half of what was accumulated at the time of the divorce. That's what the QDRO says." During his divorce, he chose not to have a lawyer who would have explained what that would mean for him.

Later, the man came to me and said that his ex-wife agreed that that wasn't right and she would do a revised QDRO. At that point I didn't know if it was even possible because she had already taken some of the money. I got the company to accept a proposed QDRO that fixed the problem and sent it to her to sign. After receiving it, she replied, "My lawyer has advised me that this is not in my best interest. I want to do the right thing, but I can't sign the revised QDRO." This caused a huge rift in the family that affected everything: their kids' weddings, who was going to pay for what, etc. He was angry because she knew what she was doing was wrong and he couldn't change this without her consent. He didn't have a leg to stand on in court because he had signed two documents that were very clear.

A few years later he came back to me and said, "We had our first grandchild and we've gotten closer and she says she's ready to move forward." That was two years ago. I prepared everything, sent it to her, and again she refused to sign it. She kept saying that she still needed a little more information. I told her, "There is no other information, the only thing we're waiting for is for you to sign this." My client is out of luck unless she changes her mind. This situation sticks with me because there is nothing I can do. Usually I can do something. Sometimes it's expensive and time consuming, but I can still do something. In this case, I couldn't do anything because he cannot force her to agree to something that's not what the original divorce agreement called for. In the meantime, he spent a lot of money trying to fix a problem that could have been prevented if he had had a divorce lawyer.

I was brought into a case several years ago. It was a simple 401(k) division, but I was brought in as part of a malpractice case. The wife's lawyer had prepared the QDRO. A lot of times people ask me, "why do I need a lawyer to do the QDRO? It's just a form and you check the boxes." The answer is because those forms are not always worded carefully; they are forms generated by the company for their convenience.

The wife's divorce lawyer had filled out a QDRO in which

the wife was supposed to get 50% of the husband's 401(k). One of the options on the form was that she would receive 50% of the marital portion of his 401(k), not 50% of the total balance. The divorce lawyer checked that box because it sounded right, both parties signed the QDRO, the judge signed it, and when the wife got her money from the 401(k), it was about $400,000 less than she was expecting. She was very upset. I actually represented the husband after the case was filed. He was generous and just wanted her to get what she was supposed to get. Most of the money in his 401(k) was premarital. The amount of money accrued in his 401(k) during their marriage was a lot less, because he had worked there a long time before the marriage. That was fixable and he was willing to fix it. I got involved when the malpractice case was filed against the wife's lawyer because she had screwed up the QDRO to begin with. In the end, the wife got her money because the husband was willing to do a revised QDRO.

Several times a week I get a phone call along the lines of: "my lawyer told me to call you because I'm getting a divorce and getting part of my husband's pension and 401(k). I don't understand why my divorce lawyer can't do this. Why do I need to pay you to do this?" My response is this: "This is an area in which the tiniest thing, like the word and in the wrong place, can make a huge difference. It's got its own separate lingo and things don't mean exactly what you think they should mean." If you don't do this regularly and don't know what to look for, you could, with all the best intentions, mess up and lose a lot of money. And there are situations, especially with pensions, where it's irrevocable and nothing can be done. That is why it is important to have either a divorce lawyer who knows what they're doing or a specialist.

Randy D. Grayson, *Litigation Attorney and Partner at DelCampo & Grayson LLC*

Many times, in a divorce, the spouse who has health insurance will agree to continue providing health insurance coverage to the spouse he or she is divorcing. Unfortunately, they make a big mistake by not telling the employer that the divorce has occurred. Under the written terms of the ERISA health insurance plan, the ex-spouse is no longer eligible to receive insurance benefits. By not informing his or her employer, they are committing insurance fraud and exposing themselves to huge problems. For example, if the divorce happened in November and a major automobile accident happened in December with $1 million in health insurance expenses, the insurer may say, "You weren't eligible at the time of these expenses and we're not covering them." So now, not only are you not following the divorce decree by providing health insurance, but you have also exposed your former spouse to $1 million in uncovered medical expenses. The correct way to handle this situation is to inform your employer and agree to pay the COBRA premiums, keeping your former spouse covered under COBRA plan.

Sherri S. Holder, *CPA/ABV/CFF, CVA, Partner at the Holder Group, LLC*

A big portion of what I do is helping people to determine the value of their assets and to prepare a marital balance sheet, in which we look at the assets and liabilities of both parties. We also look at both parties' income. Similar to the income statement of a business, we put together a financial statement for marriage dissolution purposes into a document referred to as a Domestic Relations Financial Affidavit.

The pressing questions we answer are how do you value your assets, and what is income? Equity type awards are tricky things to value. When you have someone who works for a publicly traded business, how do we value restricted stock units? How do we value stock options? How do we divide those when oftentimes they're not transferable? On the flip side, how do you deal with those as income?

In a divorce, we typically have two factors that we're looking at: income for one is alimony and the other is child support. When you're dealing with equity awards that will be future income, it can get really tricky. In the case of small business owners who have spent their lives building a business and are now divorcing, and only one of them is going to keep the business, we have a lot of issues with determining what the business is worth, and what's fair and equitable for one party to receive from that business. Another, emerging aspect that causes a lot of conflict is if the business predates the marriage. If one individual or both individuals worked in the business during the marriage, you can make what's called a separate property claim. This says that a portion of the business remains the separate property of the individual who brought it to the marriage. Then we do an analysis referred to as a Passive Active Appreciation Analysis, in which we try to determine how much of the appreciation of that business was due to marital efforts of one of the parties versus market forces or the efforts of a third party. It's an emerging area that over the last few years has become much more prominent in family law cases. Currently it is kind of a case by case basis.

Another problem we see in some divorce situations, is that there's another person being paid for by the marital estate. We often see ATM codes that appear on bank statements related to strip clubs. Unfortunately, there is an epidemic of people spending money on someone outside their marriage. We've had cases that involve sugar daddies and lots of money being paid to strippers. If the wife has a suspicion, we'll work with her to go through their credit cards. If we do find proof of her suspicions, these situations often end in divorce, depending to what degree this is happening. We have had cases when one spouse has spent $400,000 or $500,000 on extramarital affairs. When that happens, we put it on the balance sheet and put it on their side of the ledger as an asset.

Depending on the size of the estate and the amount of money spent on affairs, we try to help people make the decision of whether or not to go down the rabbit hole of sifting through those expenses and itemizing them. I had a case where the individual with bad conduct came to me and said, "Here is all my stuff and I'll tell you certain charges that I shouldn't have made. But I want you to add it up, because my wife thinks it's $1 million and it's really only about $500,000."

It's terrifying. For one, you've lost your partner. You've lost your security. Oftentimes that non-working spouse has taken the backseat on financial matters, and they are lacking that skill set to run their lives. They made a decision at whatever point and cannot go back and change that decision. Most likely, depending on their age when the divorce happens, they will never recover the money they could have made during those non-working years. However, sometimes what they get out of the divorce is more than they would have earned. It is very hard to step back into the professional life you had before choosing to stop working. There are some success stories of people who have a great career after getting divorced.

My advice to people would be, never get out of the game. Keep working in one way or another. If you were a teacher, keep substituting. If you unfortunately find yourself in a divorce situation, surround herself with an educated team and listen to them. Your team may include a great attorney, a great therapist, or even a forensic accountant. The worst thing most people go through in their life is divorce. It's the death of a spouse, but you still have to look at them and you may have to see them with their new person. It's a horrific experience and it's emotional. But if you surround yourself with a good team and let them help you with the financial aspects and listen to them, things will be okay. I think you do yourself a disservice if you don't let somebody help you with that process.

Another emerging issue we've seen in the last few years is trusts. One spouse sets up a trust and they may be the grantor of that trust or their spouse may be the grantor of the trust. Sometimes we see cases when the non-informed spouse just signs it because their husband or wife put a piece of paper in front of them. Many times these trusts have provisions that the moment that the parties are separated, no longer living together, or a divorce has been filed, that the other spouse is no longer a beneficiary of that trust. If that trust is irrevocable, oftentimes it's outside the marital state, and so they can't benefit from the trust. Suddenly a large portion of the marital assets that they've enjoyed during their marriage are no longer considered for equitable division and they've given up rights. We have seen a lot of litigation in the last four or five years over this issue. More and more often trust attorneys come in as a part of the divorce team. Sometimes, much of the legal costs deal with the trust issue.

So what I would say is, if your spouse asks you to sign something, know what you're signing; whether it's your tax return, a legal document, or a trust. Make sure that you understand if you're giving up any rights. All too often we have clients who say, "I've never actually seen my tax return. I just signed the piece of paper they gave me." And then, come to find out, there's fraud going on in the tax return. If the uninformed spouse had ever looked at it and examined their lifestyle, they would have realized they were reporting $100,000 of taxable income when their vacations cost $100,000. Know what you're signing. Your spouse may have good intentions, but you need to be an adult and be informed of whatever it is you're signing.

Rob Tamburri, *CPA and Managing Partner at Balog & Tamburri, CPAs*

Whether clients are middle class, upper class, or even wealthy, the most pressing issue couples who are divorcing face are finances. Typically one spouse doesn't have the financial savviness related to the family assets or the understanding of the tax consequences of their divorce. Unfortunately, due to the emotions of the divorce, the spouses typically have a short term financial strategy, not realizing that what they may not have now impacts what they're going to get in the future.

One great example of this is retirement money. The people getting divorced are concerned with what is happening now and not thinking about the future. If the couple tends to be older when they get divorced, one party often has a greater retirement. The other party will not have the ability to earn those retirement dollars, because it's a function of time. So what will happen down the road? Retirement monies are not dollar for dollar, it could be sixty or sixty-five cents on the dollar depending on your tax rate. All dollars are not equal. One other thing I see as well in retirement account settlements is that even if you get a QDRO, a Qualified Domestic

Relations Order, you can take some of that money now without penalty. They give you some money to live while you're looking for a job or trying to get your life organized.

Another big issue divorcing couples may not understand is that there are tax consequences to alimony and child support. The good news is that starting last year, under the Trump administration, alimony is no longer taxable to the recipient. This allows for additional negotiations during the divorce. One other thing to understand is that these rules change. For example, for years the question for tax purposes was: who was claiming the children? Under the new laws, there are no personal exemptions and instead now there are child credits. So it's very important to understand that you need to speak with a qualified tax professional or CPA to learn how the divorce settlement will impact your cash flow.

I have a couple of cases in which I helped divorcing people. If you are married, the first $500,000 of gain is tax free now. But if you get divorced, that cuts to $250,000. The spouse who's going to get the home in that settlement may find out pretty quickly that he or she can't afford the house. I would recommend keeping both names on the house until the property is sold. This way both parties avoid the tax and get that $500,000 exclusion.

Recently a female client came in to see me who was going through a divorce and she wanted me to look at the prepared settlement offer. She was hoping that I wasn't going to like it and that I could do more for her. I actually told her that the deal was very good, but I didn't like the fact that it was very back ended, that a big part of her settlement was going to be down the road. My concern was that she would never see that money. She assured me that she would because her ex-husband would become a CEO one day and she was willing to wait. I told her I didn't like the sound of it and advised her to take a little less now and be done with her obligation of having to receive money from her ex-husband. Low and behold, he lost his job. That would have impacted his ability to get some of those other assets from the company during the divorce. Everyone gets on with their life. It's better to just get the money now.

During a divorce, people are afraid. They ask themselves, can I really afford my lifestyle after my divorce? Lifestyles often change for both spouses. Typically, the wife wants to maintain the home and wants the house in the divorce. A lot of times, we can work that out. But as I mentioned before, people don't always understand the costs that are involved in maintaining an asset. Even if one spouse gets the house in the divorce, it's not free; there are HOA fees, homeowners insurance, maintenance, property taxes, and it could still cost thousands of dollars per month just to keep the house. They learn very quickly that they can't afford the home and they have to sell it. The reality is that the spouse who earns less shouldn't be interested in the house. They should be focused on retirement assets because that's what gives them long-term production. With retirement assets, people who work have the ability to fill their silos annually; there's only so much retirement money you can earn, even if you have a high paying job. The key is to protect the future and then figure out the present in a more cost-effective way.

Another concern is if one of the spouses is a business owner. This becomes an emotional issue if the other spouse wants a piece of that business. That is rarely a good idea. What I recommend is to get an evaluation of the business and pay off the other spouse. Rarely do you want your former spouse being part of your business. They may not have the management ability to run the business or the employees may not even like the spouse. I have seen many examples where the former spouse does get part of the business and it ends up going out of business a couple years later.

Tax returns are another issue to consider. One of the most common things we see is when a couple is separated or is in the process of separating and taxes are due and they want to file. I often get phone calls from clients in this situation who want to file separately because they want to begin to distance themselves from their spouse. Nine times out of ten, that's a very poor decision. It's very expensive because under most circumstances, when a couple files jointly, they reduce their tax bill. That is a benefit because one of those additional tax savings can help pay for the attorney and they will also have the assets to divide. One exception is if a spouse does have their own business or if one spouse is concerned that something is going on with that business that may be unethical, clients need to remember that if you sign a joint return, you're both equally obligated to pay that tax and are responsible for any problems on that return. There is something called innocent spouse relief, but it is a complicated process.

Andy Flink, *Founder at Flink Family Law Mediation/Arbitration*

Typically, when I meet people in mediation, they're good people going through a very difficult time in their lives. So I would have to say that the biggest challenge is getting people to think along the lines of how does this legal process work? What does the end result look like? What's the range of settlement as opposed to how they personally feel about what the other spouse did or didn't do that led them to a divorce.

What people think they should get, and what the legal system decides they get are two very different things. I will say that there are compartments to that. The first one is that not all decisions and positions that parties take in mediation are financial positions. Meaning, if a party feels as though they were the ones wronged, they're looking for some sort of pay-back. Their intent is that this person did so many bad things that they should pay for their actions. However, the courts typically are not moved by emotion. As an individual who went through divorce myself, I can tell you that that meant a whole lot to me when I was going through it. A thousand plus mediations later, it doesn't mean a whole lot to me. As a matter of fact, I'm more surprised when I don't hear about conduct issues. People are often hyper-focused on what they think the outcome of mediation should be, not necessarily what the outcome will be based on what the court will do. It's important to focus on what the court will do because that's the last stop. We use that as a basis to determine the range of what can we settle on, and what will most likely get parties into that range of settlement.

Often, people have no idea what they do and do not have. Most couples that come into mediation aren't walking in there with a marital balance sheet that explains all of their assets and liabilities. It's a very murky and cloudy area. What the couple has acquired during the marriage is what is subject to division. People don't focus on that and most of the time if one party has a good beat on what that is, typically they have not shared it with the other party.

I see difference between men and women in their approach to mediation. Not to be stereotypical, but I see a lot of cases where men have been moving up the corporate ladder for years and the spouse is more of the caretaker of the children. She is not necessarily as focused on the career as he is. Let's say a party is married for twenty years and they have two teenage kids. The mom has not really worked, while dad has worked more than twenty years, acquiring a good salary with bonuses and stock option. I personally feel that her role in the family is just as important, if not more so than his role in the family. When he says in mediation: "I earned it, why should I divide it?" The reality is that he couldn't do what he was doing if she wasn't doing what she was doing. The parties basically have an agreement where this is the role he is going to play and this is the role that she is going to play. The person who earned the money does not have the right to say "I earned it, you didn't earn it." This is also the point in a divorce when the husband typically says, "she can go out and work, I'm not paying for her alimony."

Assuming that the kids will eventually age out in a short period of time, in three to five years, even at that point, the person who is the stay-at-home parent will most likely never earn more than maybe 10 to 15% of what the working spouse will earn over the following ten years, no matter how capable they are.

I always find that the devil is in the details. You have to dot every i and cross every t as a family law mediator. If you look at all issues from a worst-case scenario perspective, you can end up with a good result. For example, if the parties are going to sell their property, they have to have terms as to when and how it's going to be sold, who's going to sell it, what offer they will take, and the lowest offer they have to take. A lot of details aren't necessarily spelled out in the parties' agreements and then it's left to them to determine what the outcome should be and that's where they fight. When parties have a disagreement on what should happen, I come in to help them as a neutral party who can offer information. I look at it from the perspective of what is going to be equally satisfactory or equally unsatisfactory to both parties to put them in a range of compromise where we can come up with something that will work. I help define the terms.

Part of the reason why this occurs is because there are a few words that go in front of any terms and conditions that we put in a document, contract, or agreement which state that unless the parties otherwise agree, the parties can agree to anything they want. The terms we put in place assume they are not going to agree on anything. For example, let's say a house is going to be sold for $400,000 and the parties must accept any asking price within 5%, or $20,000, meaning that the parties have to accept any offer of $380,000 or higher. If somebody offers them $385,000, by contract, they must take that. However, they can also jointly agree and say, "we just listed it today, it's our first offer, it came in 20 minutes after we put it on realtor.com, so we want to wait." They have the ability to make choices like that, but we always assume that people are not going to agree on anything because it is a divorce. We give them defined terms and parameters, which are very important.

When I see most mistakes by people is, in a generalized statement, that most people live 20% beyond their means. For example, let's say the household income is X during the year and they live at X plus 20%. Then, in March of the subsequent year, one of the working spouses receives their bonus for his/her performance the prior year and they use that bonus to pay off whatever debt they have accrued of that 20%. Then the cycle starts all over again. One problem is that sometimes that bonus doesn't come. Another problem is people typically don't have an idea of what they do and do not have. By virtue of a divorce, two households are going to cost more than one. The most extreme examples are the parties who have $3 million worth of assets and $100,000 worth of credit card debt that they continue to make minimum payments on. I always like to say, "I'm going to show you how you can make 21% on your money and pay off your credit cards." But people don't have a focus and have a tendency to overlook very, very important details that I think are easily fixable.

Divorce can be one of the lowest times in a person's life. When they come to see me, they may have unrealistic expectations, not understanding how complicated it can be. I try to help them with equitable division. That typically means 50/50, but it's always subject to other percentages, such as 60/40 or 55/45. Ultimately, that can only be decided by a court unless it's agreed to by the parties in a process like mediation. What I try to tell people is to look at the finances.

Let's say that both parties are on a seesaw and each party makes the same amount of money, $100,000 a year income, so the seesaw is even. But let's say one party makes $450,000 a year and the other party makes $15,000 a year, you can see that the Seesaw is way out of whack. So what we try to do is use the ingredients of income and equitable division to try to get that seesaw as close to even as we can. In a divorce, there are two households, so all the money, instead of coming into one, has to go into two. Sometimes it's even, sometimes one household gets a little more than the other. That may be factored in if they're doing a custody arrangement and have minor children, then it's not a 50/50 arrangement. All those factors are taken into consideration in trying to get that seesaw level.

Deborah Wilder, PhD, *Psychologist, Divorce Mediator, Divorce Counselor and Parenting Coordinator at the Center for Therapy and Mediation*

In the divorce community, I think the biggest element is fear. Fear about the children being okay emotionally, mentally, and physically. Then of course there is fear when it comes to finances. Unfortunately, many times, children tend to be collateral damage as far as the fallout from divorce, not always, but it is a concern. Financially, even those people who make a good living, when moving from one house to two houses, can have a difficult time. The main concern is making sure that there is enough money now, and in the future, and being able to live a quality life while providing for the children.

People have the most financial issues with the fear of whether or not they will have enough money that will cover their bills. Will there be enough money to allow the kids to play sports and get tutoring if they need, and even to have some extra? And then of course, the fear of being able to manage all of this?

Many times those women are busy running around taking the kids here and there and do not really have time to deal with the finances. And that is in no way a reflection of their intelligence. In a relationship with a husband and a wife, oftentimes, the husband will bring in more. Just to be clear, this is not always the case, I'm just generalizing. Sometimes the women may even decide to give up a job and a career in order to stay home and raise the children. I'm big on identifying working outside of the home versus working inside of the home. When you work inside of the home, you don't get a paycheck, but you work very hard raising the children and managing the home, which is hard work. A lot of times when people get divorced, the women especially struggle with that because they have given up an income and at the time both parties decided that that was the way it was going to be. Sadly, sometimes it bites them when divorce happens because now they've got to start over while still raising the kids if they are young. They wonder how they are going to manage working while still doing carpool. This is in your typical standard divorce versus a divorce among couples who generally get along better and share custody and parenting.

When I got divorced, my kids were young. I didn't want them to be upset and I didn't want them to be in pain. I was hurt when they were hurt and it was such a struggle, so I would buy them things. If they wanted video games and they worked hard in school work, most of the time I would say yes. This was not a reflection on them. They didn't want anything unusual, but I said yes and unfortunately was not good at managing my money and staying within a budget. So one of the challenges for parents, either moms or dads, is being careful while making financial decisions. We don't want our children to feel hurt or upset, and we may make decisions based off of that. Not all parents struggle with this, but many do. In the long run, these are not good habits to have.

When I realized that I was spending more to satisfy the children's emotional needs and didn't have that kind of money, I used credit cards. It's interesting because one of my kids (he's now 21) said to me a couple of years ago, "Mom, you did that for you." And it's true, I did. I got them things or tried to satisfy their immediate needs because I was uncomfortable with their discomfort. I'm a psychologist. I thought to myself, why didn't I think of that?

I told him he was absolutely right. I have a very hard time when my kids are uncomfortable or are in pain. But they could have dealt with it. It wasn't anything bad. It wasn't like I was depriving them of anything they needed. Ultimately, it was me putting my own needs onto them. My kids knew that the intentions of my actions were good, but the reality was that they would have been fine even without getting these little things. And in my financial situation at the time, I did not have the structure and commitment to stay within a budget.

Kids are resilient and much stronger than we think. And the best thing that parents can do for their children going through a divorce is to avoid having conflict in front of the children. It's not about the money for them. The worst thing that can happen is for the kids to see the parents fighting and not working through it. That's different to say if there's an argument, children can see if you resolve it in a healthy way and then you're teaching them how to resolve problems too. But if it's just conflict without resolution, and the kids are getting sucked into the mess, that's bad.

A lot of women struggle and try to remarry so that they can be more financially stable with two incomes. But the second marriage divorce rates are even higher rate than first marriage divorces. The divorce rate for first marriages is even going down a bit and I think it is because people are waiting longer to get married, first establishing their own careers. This results in them having children later as well. The divorce rate of the second marriages is maybe 70 to 75%. Sometimes we bring to our next relationship what we didn't work through in our first marriage. There also is the aspect that some people just don't want to be alone so they may rush into something. Sometimes the new spouse also has children, which complicates the marriage. It is so difficult to blend two families together.

I work with many women, some men too, in which a spouse will try to use intimidation to threaten against divorced: she will get nothing except child support if she seeks divorce. He may tell her that he earned all the money and therefore it is his. The reality is that that is not true. Everything that is acquired and any debt that they have together is marital, but a lot of people don't know that and are afraid to leave their spouse.

I worked with a woman who had two teenage daughters and she had given up a career to raise the children because that's what both partners had decided. And it worked out very well. The husband made a good living and when they were getting a divorce, he was a bully, telling her that she needed to go back to work. It is very important for people going through this to know what their rights are and to know that the more knowledge you have, the more power you have, so that you can't be bullied or intimidated. I helped ease her mind a little bit and get advice and guidance from an attorney and from financial professionals who knew what they were talking about so she didn't have to go into this divorce petrified that she would not make it.

1. Don't move out of your house too quickly during divorce if you want to be involved in parenting after the divorce.

2. Don't let your educational credentials expire. You don't know when death, disability, or divorce may happen with your spouse.

3. The dollar amount you receive in retirement accounts is pre-tax, so remember that the value you receive will be 35% to 40% less.

4. Once you agree on the alimony amount from your ex-spouse, it's non-modifiable. This is also true for some retirement accounts that are not divisible. Hire a professional before you agree to anything.

5. If you keep a house and refinance the mortgage after the divorce, make sure you qualify for the loan by yourself. It's not free to keep a house. If possible, sell it while you can get a bigger exemption.

6. Many times, men control the finances, especially in a longer marriage, which makes women unaware of their own financial information. Participate in your own family finances.

7. Don't mingle your inheritance with your spouse. Don't put it in a joint account. If you keep it separate and get divorce, it's all yours.

8. If you have a blended marriage, think through the situation after your death and make sure to have a will.

9. Be very careful of technology since it can trip you up if you are hiding information from your spouse. Change login information for everything that you created for you and your spouse before.

10. Don't put too much information in the documents that become public.

11. It's rarely a good idea to file taxes separately while you are in the process of separating or getting a divorce. File jointly. Reducing your tax bill helps pay for the attorneys and you will have another asset to divide.

12. If your health insurance covers your former spouse, after the divorce he or she is ineligible to receive benefits. Inform your employer of your divorce and agree to pay the COBRA premiums to cover the ex-spouse.

What's Your Money Story? Find out: **www.ChooseYourMoneyStory.com**

CHAPTER TWO

Inheritance

"The rich invest in time, the poor invest in money."

—WARREN BUFFET

TWENTY PERCENT OF BABY BOOMERS believe they'll receive money from parents or other relatives.[1] There are many articles about Baby Boomers, born between 1946 and 1964, who, as a group, will inherit trillions from their parents. However, according to AARP, the average inheritance received in 2016 amounted to $48,000.[2] While it's true that Baby Boomers' parents built up sizable nest eggs over the last several decades, longer life-expectancies, soaring healthcare costs, long-term care costs, and, more recently, the poor economy has wiped away these nest eggs.

Nearly 70% of millennials expect an inheritance, yet only 40% of their parents have planned to leave one.[3] A major part of this shift away from leaving an inheritance is due to the

---

1. Schwab, October 10, 2019
2. babyboomer-magazine.com
3. Natixis U.S. Investor Survey, August 22, 2018

same causes that have drained Baby Boomers' inheritances. Solution? Instead of counting on a large inheritance, begin saving your own money.

HELEN S-D'S STORY:
Don't Use All of Your Cash

I was 28 years old when my mother died of breast cancer, three years after my dad had passed away from a second massive heart attack. I met my first husband six months prior to my dad's death. Looking back, I felt that God brought Henry into my life because I was about to lose both of my parents within three years.

When my mom passed, of course, I took care of everything with the finances and medical decisions, since she gave me the Power of Attorney. We had an attorney who took care of settling the estate. My brother, David, and I were each left 50% of the life insurance. With the inheritance, my husband and I bought a house together. I was very proud that I could do that. We renovated the house together and then sold it and moved to Atlanta. When we moved, we purchased a franchise called Super Coups with my inheritance. It was a coupon company. We did not do our due diligence unfortunately and we found out the hard way that there were too many advertisers in Atlanta. We got incorporated in 1992. In 1996, only four years later, Atlanta held the Olympics. Everyone was coming to Atlanta thinking that they could make a living. We had too many advertisers and too many competitors. We were naive as entrepreneurs—we should never ever have tried to run a business so soon after buying a house and moving to a new city.

We did the best we could, but unfortunately the money ran out. Finally, my husband wanted to leave, end the business, and move to Florida. So, we parted ways. We wanted different things in life and so we got divorced. I didn't want to hold him back. I wanted to continue with my marketing company. I was stubborn and selfish and in denial.

Unfortunately, I came across a lot more problems. A lot of people that I put on retainer with deposits, later cheated me and would not pay their final bills. The lesson I learned was that I should have always gotten a 100% payment upfront. Some of my clients would pay 25% or 50% and then run off and not pay the rest. I took them to Magistrate's Court, won my case, but still they wouldn't pay me. They had many excuses. I should have hired the right people to help me.

My hardships in business were due to the fact that I trusted people too much, I couldn't afford to do many of the procedures correctly, and I couldn't afford to hire the right people. I think these are very important lessons. Young entrepreneurs should do their due diligence and homework ahead of time.

I find that people don't always recognize their needs. I needed to put aside proper savings at that time. I should have invested more wisely. In the end I declared bankruptcy. Then I looked for a job with benefits, and I made a very nice living. I started paying off my debt, started realizing that I was not experienced enough as an entrepreneur, and needed a proper job with employer benefits such as health insurance and retirement plans.

AUTHOR'S NOTES

Helen bought her first house and the business with her first husband with the inheritance money from her parents. She didn't think about savings at that time, even though her parents taught her to do so.

If she had had a Financial Planner back then, they would have recommended that she put a certain percentage of the house price in savings, and start the business with down payments and financed the rest after calculating her cash flow including income and expenses. When people start a brand-new business, they should decide up front the maximum amount of money they can invest into it and not go over that amount. Helen should have kept one or two years of expenses in savings as rainy day money when starting her new business and invested the rest for her retirement and her individual investment accounts.

Helen did not separate her inheritance from her first husband as she should have. Instead, they used it to buy a house and business together. That was a big mistake that she could have avoided by not co-mingling her inheritance and by putting it into her own individual account.

DARREN'S STORY:

Select Your Beneficiary Carefully

Darren came to my office after he had inherited money from his brother's life insurance policy. Darren's brother, Adam, his spouse, and their two children ages six and eight, were in a car accident. Adam, who was driving, missed an exit off the highway and ran into a guardrail. Adam and his spouse died immediately, but miraculously, their two children in the back survived.

Darren said that he wanted to invest the money for his retirement. I asked him, "What's the purpose of the money? Why did Adam name you as a beneficiary of the life insurance policy?"

Darren replied, "My brother wanted me and my wife to take care of his children in case he and his wife died."

"If that's the case, you need to use the money to take care of his children," I said.

Darren insisted, however, that his parents had decided to take care of the children so the money was his. He said that he would not give any of the money to his parents for the children.

I decided not to take him as a client.

AUTHOR'S NOTES

Darren's brother, Adam, put his wife as a primary beneficiary of the life insurance policy and put Darren as a contingent beneficiary. Since Adam's wife also died at the same time, the insurance money went to Darren, the contingent beneficiary. Since their parents were older, Adam assumed that Darren and his wife would take care of his children.

The best thing Adam could have done would have been to create a trust to benefit his children. The life insurance proceeds would go to the trust to be used for their health, maintenance of their lifestyle, their education, and their support until they became adults. However, many people hesitate to go to a lawyer and draft a trust due to the cost. Also, they assume that both spouses will not die at the same time.

Adam also should have discussed his life insurance policy with Darren to make sure that the proceeds should be used for his children, not for Darren's retirement.

WISDOM FROM THE EXPERTS AND PROFESSIONALS

Linda Klein, *former President of the American Bar Association, the first woman President of the State Bar of Georgia, and senior managing shareholder at the Baker Donelson law firm*

On the subject of estate plans, I think of a story of a husband and wife who were married for more than fifty years. The wife worked in the family business, so she wasn't the typical stay at home mom like June Cleaver in *Leave it to Beaver*. She helped her husband grow the business and when he passed away all of the money was put into a trust. The children were made the trustees. In violation of the trust and in violation of tax law, they didn't give their mother any money. This is a situation in which a husband and wife planned for the future. They had an estate plan that was, by all stretches of the imagination, a good one from a tax avoidance standpoint. Their children, however, who should have been taking care of their mother, refused to do it. Mark Twain once said, "You never really know someone until you share an inheritance with them." This is an example of that truth.

If you're inheriting cash outright, choosing to spend it all is not a good idea. Remember that someone left you that money because they wanted it to be your nest egg.

Laurie Dyke, *CPA, Managing Partner at IAG Forensics & Valuation*

In cases involving estates and trusts, as well as divorce, women tend to trust their family members and don't always verify the information they're given. For example, a man dies and leaves a trust for his wife, the mother of his children, and puts an adult child as the trustee of the trust. But the child may be under financial pressure. They may feel burdened by having to take care of the elderly mother. And, all too often they help themselves to the trust. The mother may feel uncomfortable about it, but does not want to disrupt the relationship. Down the road this ends in a big, very expensive investigation, when it is discovered that the trustee has taken assets they were not entitled to.

As Ronald Reagan said, "Trust but Verify."

David Golden, *Estate and Tax Attorney and Partner at Trout-man Pepper Hamilton Sanders LLP*

In the case of an inheritance of a closely held business, the big issues typically revolve around how the owner is going to leave that business. One issue I typically see in family businesses, is if there are some family members who are part of the business, employees of business, who may in fact already have an ownership interest in the business. Do you leave it to all the children even though some are not involved in the business? And how do you structure that transition? That can be a big problem that I try to help people with. From an estate tax perspective, one concern is whether the business is valued as such that passing it on to children will attract a state tax and how to deal with the estate tax. If you have a spouse, you can defer the tax, but you will have to deal with the state taxes.

My advice in that situation is to leave the business to the people who are going to be working in the business. If it is at all possible, leave that value to them. Compensate the other members of the family with other assets and make up the difference with insurance if the client is insurable. In my experience, it is a mistake to leave a business by dividing between children who are not involved in the business along with children who are involved. Typically, the kids who are not involved in the business and are not drawing a salary come to resent their siblings for taking a salary. They feel they should get some sort of benefit from the business. They want some sort of dividends. The children who are involved in the business generally want to keep profits in the business. They can expand the business with the profits and are rarely interested in paying dividends. This causes a lot of tension. My advice is to try to avoid that tension by leaving other assets to the children who aren't involved in the business.

What happens to the children who are not involved in the business and who do not receive equity? Can they try to get more money in the future if the business is sold for more than the current value? Well, no. The rationale is that they got their part of the estate. That's fixed. The business, in most cases, grew because of the people who were running it. They created that value and it's only fair they should benefit from their hard work.

Let's say that the estate is composed of a business worth $50 million and other assets worth $5 million. Typically, most entrepreneurs view their businesses as their retirement plan and don't have a lot of equity outside of the businesses. If it's not possible to leave equal assets to the children who are not involved in the business, the next best thing is to create two classes of stock—two types of membership interest: voting and non-voting. Give the non-voting interest to the beneficiaries who are not involved in the business and the voting interest to the beneficiaries who are involved. That at least consolidates the decision making and the people who are involved in the business. You still have some pressure with respect to distribution and such, but beneficiaries who are not involved in the business don't have a right to vote. They have limited rights with respect to the business. If there is tension, the voting shareholders can figure out some way to buy out the non-voting shareholders. This can create tension and financial strain on the business, but that's better than simply dividing the business equally.

I had a situation in which the dad started a business. He had four children: two girls and two boys. The two girls were involved in the business. The boys were not involved in the business. The business was left to the mom who then left it equally to all four of the children. Over time there was tension between the beneficiaries who were not involved in the business and the beneficiaries who were involved. The beneficiaries who were not involved wanted to benefit from the business because their family had started the business; their name was on the business. Yet, they were getting nothing. The people involved in the business were trying to grow the business. Whatever extra they had, they put back into the business to make it more valuable. Eventually it became so contentious that they ended up selling the business. They couldn't resolve the tensions and it was easier to sell. There were other reasons to sell as well, but that was one of the motivating factors. This case shows that, unless you plan properly, leaving a business as an inheritance can jeopardize the long-term plan and family ties.

Business owners with valuable business often worry about how they're going to pay estate tax without having to sell the business. There are some provisions in the internal revenue code in which you can pay the tax over time, up to 15 years if you qualify. I recommend that people who are young enough and insurable, set up a life insurance policy. This is not subject to estate tax and that money can provide liquidity for the business. A valuable business can keep people up at night worrying about estate taxes. While they don't affect many people, they can hit you pretty hard at 40%.

I have a situation now in which the kids own a majority of the business. The mom owns a minority. She is aging and is determined to equally divide her stock among her children, and is not interested in any sort of voting or non-voting. It's a successful business and there will be tension between the children who have a relatively small interest. They're going to want dividends and they'll have to try to work something out with their siblings. What you hope over time is they get along and not get involved in sibling rivalries. The hope is that they can work out a fair buy-out strategy. Unfortunately buyouts can be contentious. If you're really doing it properly and someone has a minority interest in a closely held business, there are discounts that are applied. Say the business is worth $10 million and they own 5% interest. Five percent of a $10 million business should mean they are owed $500,000. However, their interest isn't worth $500,000. It's reduced because there's a lack of control, lack of marketability in a family setting.

Don Deloach, *Estate Planning Attorney at Caldwell, Propst & DeLoach, LLP*

Many people with considerable wealth who come to my office have no wills, no trust, and no planning for their future. Sometimes their wills are old and inadequate. The documents that they created twenty or twenty-five years ago don't fit in their current situation anymore and need an update. They see many wills that people have done by themselves or online. Many times, the survivors are women. But often these women simply have no clue about what they had with their spouse or how to manage the money they've inherited, since the spouse took care of all the financial affairs.

Estate tax laws have changed radically in the past ten to twenty years and many people no longer need elaborative and complicated wills and trusts. In the 1980s and 1990s, there were concerns on estate tax because of the lower exemption amount. But now, the concerns have been shifted more to income tax planning, such as making sure to take a step-up basis at death. Most people can simplify their old and complicated wills.

I recall a situation in which my client was on his way to a long international vacation. The day before the trip, he called me. The man and his wife didn't have the chance to go to his office to sign their wills. The client said that his son would sign their wills as one of the witnesses. Don said, "No, your son will be disqualified from receiving anything if he signs and you die."

I often see no residual clause in wills that were done by attorneys who do not specialize in trusts and estates. This is a serious defect. Other mistakes that people often make is making a second or the third spouse together with a child from a previous marriage co-trustees. People do this often without thinking, since their current spouse and child from a previous marriage get along really well. However this cordial relationship often ends in a disastrous situation.

CHAPTER **TWO** SUMMARY

1. People tend to believe they are invincible after receiving an inheritance and want to acquire something with it. Instead of spending it all, add the money to your retirement accounts.

2. If you do choose to spend it, go to your financial planner and make a life plan. Once the money is spent, it's gone forever.

3. Get involved in your family finances from the beginning. If something unexpected happens, you will have an easier transition.

4. Make sure you separate your inheritance from your spouse. Don't put it in a joint account.

5. If you have minor children, create a trust and make them the beneficiaries. A guardian should be a trustee, not a beneficiary.

6. When you create a trust and name your adult children as trustees, instead of your spouse who is a beneficiary of the trust, consider it from a tax standpoint and provide flexibility to your beneficiary or if appropriate, include your spouse as co-trustee.

7. If you are the beneficiary and someone else is the trustee, verify the information you are given about the trust. Also, do not blindly trust a family member. If that person has been dishonest in the past, do not trust the person with your money.

8. When leaving your family business to your children, give it to those who are involved in the business. Give other assets to the children who are not in the business to avoid conflicts among siblings.

9. Make sure that you have a will. If you did your will by yourself or used online materials, it may not be valid in your state. Also update your will every several years.

10. Avoid partnering your children from a previous marriage and your current spouse as co-trustees. Their interests are vastly different.

What's Your Money Story? Find out: **www.ChooseYourMoneyStory.com**

CHAPTER THREE

Retirement

*"The question isn't at what age I want
to retire, it's at what income."*

—GEORGE FOREMAN

FORTY-SEVEN PERCENT OF BABY BOOMERS, born between 1946 and 1964, are already in retirement. Three main sources of income for retirees are Social Security, private pensions, and personal savings. But as a nation, no one is in great shape. The average Social Security check is $14,000 a year. Less than one quarter of younger boomers have a private company pension plan. Forty-five percent of Boomers have zero savings for retirement.[1] In addition, most retirees have not thought about the cost of long-term care, since they plan to rely on Medicare. However, Medicare provides virtually no coverage for long-term care.

Among all married couples over 65, one of the pair will likely survive to at least 95. It's important to plan now and begin saving more systematically while thinking about reducing expenses. Delayed gratification will work for you in the end.

---

1. www.cnbc.com, April 9, 2019

ANNETTE'S STORY:

Save the Maximum to Enjoy Later

I worked for a world professional services firm for over 25 years and then retired. My pension started at age 60, but without receiving it, I've been managing and enjoying my life from my savings.

It was a tough decision. I actually thought about retiring earlier, when I was feeling a little burnt out. My health was suffering, and it took more and more energy to work at full speed. So, I decided that I wanted to make a change. Instead of focusing on client transformations, mergers, divestitures, and shared services—all the things that I did as a consultant and a partner—I started focusing a little bit more on myself. I began discussing my future with a financial advisor about four years before I actually retired. The advisor and I decided that I needed to wait at least two years for a greater comfort level to retire. As I got closer to the time, I made sure that I wouldn't have to work another day in my life. I had enough runway. My financial plan was to live until I was a hundred, which I will do. Even living to a hundred, I wanted to have money to give to people I care about, a charity, a trust or whatever.

Now, I'm looking at the numbers and everything looks too good to be true. I'm too young. My advisor said, "well, this is possible even with fairly conservative assumptions." Now that I'm more confident and comfortable with the way things are going and the way I have been living, I'm starting to talk with my advisor about doing much more risky things. The first couple of years after retirement, I was in a little bit of shock wondering if this was just a dream or if it was real. This is awesome. I have a great life now and I'm healthier and happier. So I'm wondering, what else can I do now? I've been on some boards and I'm looking at some angel investing and a couple of things like that. I have room to do this in my portfolio. I want to make smart decisions about money and I don't want to go crazy risky. So, I will invest in a female entrepreneur or something that I'm really passionate about. I could help others with their businesses and use my business, consulting, strategy, and operation background.

Some people ask me whether I had an identity crisis after I retired. I can answer that in two ways. Before I retired, I felt so tied to my work and my firm. Even my family would say that I was married to work. I wanted to change that and be known for something else. I worked really hard on that. After I retired, it was pure joy to not have a calendar that I had to follow. The calendar was a choice. Sleeping in, enjoying a cup of coffee, having "me-time," I have more choices now. I can run an errand on a Wednesday versus running on a Saturday when I had no time. Going somewhere on a Wednesday looks very different—no one's there—than when I did my groceries on the weekend. It's a calmer life. I can do more exercising and I have better health. I can also travel more. I do a couple of trips every year. In fact, this year I got forty people to go to a health resort with me. There's one in Tucson, one in California, one in Austin, and one in Mexico.

My advice to other people is to have conversations early with a good financial advisor that you trust. Search around for one that you connect with and feel comfortable with and who takes you seriously. The other thing is to be more mindful of how you spend your discretionary time and money. Live below your means and save more. Any time the firm I worked for offered something in which there was any kind of contribution, I maxed it out. I maxed it out from day one and that's what I tell other people to do too.

I have a lot of options in the future. One is a long-term care insurance. If something happens to me from a health standpoint, I'm taken care of—probably better than I am now. Right now, I don't even have all my options turned on. I don't have the pension turned on. I don't have Social Security turned on. I have some annuities that aren't turned on yet. I'm living off of the investment earnings now, which is pretty much what I had before I retired and invested.

AUTHOR'S NOTES

It's impressive that Annett was able to retire after working and saving for 25 years. She is not taking pensions and Social Security retirement benefit and has been using her savings to retire early. It's important to save the maximum amount each year in your retirement accounts from an early age if you can. Take advantage of the compounding effect of the money and start early!

Due to her discipline, she can really enjoy her life. For Annett, work became a choice, not a necessity.

ALAN'S STORY:

Missing the Game

I had my business, "Tower East, Beer, Wine and Spirits." The reason we called it Tower East was because it was located in East Atlanta. I first retired about five and a half years ago. I didn't have to go to work and I didn't have to go to the store. I was probably one of the happiest men on the planet. It felt great. It was a load of pressure off me. The business I was in was a tough business. It was successful and lucrative, but not easy. It was located in a tough, gentrified neighborhood. It was a little more challenging when I first bought the business: there was an incident every hour, there was always something going on. It was hard to manage business. Losses started to change and continued to change. It became harder. Then somebody knocked on the door and gave me an offer that I couldn't refuse.

I put together my own advisory board. I had a lawyer and I talked to other people who had done business with the people who wanted to buy the business. We struck a deal and took the offer. That's the short version of the story. It was easier said than done. The deal began in February and it really didn't end till August. There was a lot to sell: a liquor store and two commercial buildings.

After the sale, I became the president of our synagogue, Congregation B'nai Torah for two years. That was full-time volunteer work, and it was very rewarding. I even got a free trip to Israel through the Jewish Federation. I met a lot of people. It was a good two years and I was successful. There was really no drama in the synagogue. The biggest challenge was renewing the Rabbi's contract. (That was about as much fun as a root canal!)

After the term as president ended, I noticed that I had a little more time on my hands. I enjoyed having lunch with people, but I missed being around people all day and waiting on customers. Even in the old stores, it's crazy, but I enjoyed waiting on some of my old customers. They used to call me Mr. Tower. I went to lunch with my stepbrother who owns two liquor stores. He said, "Why don't you help out for the holidays, Thanksgiving, Christmas, and New Year?" Those are the big sales times outside of Super Bowl weekend. He said, "Just work in the liquor department, sell scotch and bourbon." So I did. It was so good waiting on customers again. Some of them were from my old store. They were just so happy to see me. The store was located in the area where I grew up and I saw people from school I hadn't seen in a long time. People in my old show business life were coming in, too. I was just having a good time; it was fun and I looked forward to it. It was nice, just selling liquor without the headache of owning the store.

I missed being in the game, I missed the wheeling and dealing, too. I was kind of kicking around the question in my head: What do I want to do now? I had been an entrepreneur or working for myself since my early 30s, now I am 68. Entrepreneurs like myself are hard workers but lousy employees. We're never good at punching a clock. Even though my hours were from 11AM to 7PM, I had the hardest time getting there in the morning. I think it's the entrepreneur spirit. Once I got there, I sold the merchandise, but I did miss the game. I kept trying to think of a way for me to get back in the game and still keep my independence.

I talked to some friends of mine. I put together my own advisory board to help me make a decision. I got together with several brothers and friends who were doing real estate and asked them about it. The idea kind of hit me because one of the guys who was working in the liquor store was also in real estate. He was younger and he was having to work forty hours a week to support his family. He was kind of new at it. There are a lot of people who work part-time jobs until they can get their real estate business going. I asked him a lot of questions and learned that I have to take a 75-hour pre-licensed course and pass the state exam in order to get my real estate license. Outside of learning the Torah with the Rabbis, the last time I took an exam was when I graduated from Georgia State University in '74. That was a long time ago.

I decided to go for it. I passed the test and am enjoying being a realtor. I may have my first listing with a guy who is going through a divorce. He's waiting on the attorney to work out the details. So once that gets worked out, that would be my first listing.

I want to continue doing this as long as I'm healthy. What's good about what I'm doing now is I can set my own hours. One of my friends said that in the real estate business, there's no ceiling but there's also no floor. What you put in is what you'll get back. In sports terms, I hope that the touch down will come soon.

AUTHOR'S NOTES

It is interesting how everyone's view of retirement is different. I hear a lot of similar stories from men. While many women enjoy going into their retirement and love to take care of their grandchildren (if any), men sometimes get bored and feel that something is missing. It happens especially for people who had wonderful careers and people around them.

You don't have to wait until you retire to find a second career. While you are working, if you don't want to retire completely, you can dream and plan for a new chapter of your life.

Many people who retire without goals or a purpose develop feelings of isolation and a loss of identity that sometimes causes depression. If you are five to ten years away from your retirement, find something you enjoy doing now. What are the things that you are really interested in but haven't had the time to do? Develop your interests and hone your skills. This could lead you to a part-time job that you will really enjoy in your retirement!

ZAHAVA AND YOSEF'S STORY:
If You Don't Start Now, When?

Advisor Rebecca received an email from Zahava who was connected to Rebecca by some friend. Zahava and her husband Yosef live in NY and have several children in private schools. Zahava is a successful doctor and has her own practice. Yosef is a home maker and has been taking care of their children. Zahava asked Rebecca for a meeting since they are in their mid-forties and have no savings whatsoever.

Rebecca agreed to meet with them for creating a retirement plan for their future. Zahava and Yosef bought their $1.2MM house a few years ago. They borrowed the $200,000 down payment money from Zahava's father and other friends and financed $1MM from a bank, therefore, they basically owe almost all the money.

Zahava's income is close to $700,000 but they have saved literally nothing due to all the costs for repayment of their house loans, children's education, therapy for some children, and all other expenses. Every year they planned to start saving but haven't been able to find money. Now they see they have been living from pay check to pay check for over fifteen years, yet they still don't know how to break the cycle.

When advisor Rebecca asked to review their expenses to access where they could cut back, Yosef got upset and told Rebecca that it was pointless to try to calculate their expenses since the number was different every month, making it silly to even try making such a plan. Advisor Rebecca told them that making a retirement plan is like creating a blue print of a house. "You cannot build your house without a blue print. You have to know where the kitchen and office will be, how many bedrooms and bathrooms you want, where a garage will be, etc. By creating a realistic plan, you can work on executing it," Rebecca explained. Yosef rolled his eyes like a teenager and stormed out of the room, claiming he needed to run an errand. Rebecca saw that though her advice was needed, it was not wanted: She charged nothing and left their house.

AUTHOR'S NOTES

If you want to retire in the future and do not have any savings, you have to make a plan and start saving right away. Otherwise, nothing will happen when you get older unless you KNOW that you will receive a handsome inheritance.

Ideally, one should save the maximum allowable amount in your retirement account. In addition, save 3-6 months of monthly net income for an emergency fund.

If Zahava had started a retirement plan such as a 401(k) plan and made Yosef as one of her employees, both of them could have saved the yearly maximum amount. By saving for the past fifteen years, they would have had probably over $1MM savings already with 7-8% annual return. With time and compound effect, a small amount of savings each year becomes a large number in the future, especially if they had begun saving when they were younger. For example, the $1MM would have doubled and become $2MM in ten years (at 7.2% annual return). Then the $2MM would have doubled to $4MM in the next ten years. In order to get the benefit of compounding, Zahava and Yosef needed to start saving early on and continue.

When you want to lose weight, you will exercise. It's the same thing for savings, and you have to work on it.

AUDREY'S STORY:

Where in the World Did My Inheritance Go?

Audrey, a sophisticated French woman, asked the author in a business networking meeting to council with her on her upcoming inheritance. Audrey told the author that her parents got a divorce "a while ago." Her father remarried, and Audrey has two step sisters. She doesn't know them very well since she lives in the U.S. and they live in France. Since her mother passed away a decade ago, she hasn't been to France so often.

In recent years, her father passed away and Audrey claims she was supposed to have a substantial inheritance from her father's estate. The author asked Andrey, "If your father passed away years ago, why do you still believe that you are getting his money? If the estate has not settled, it must certainly be close to settling, and you should have had definitive info about the estate if you are involved."

Audrey said, "My father's estate was large and it takes time to divide it among the beneficiaries. Once I get my share, I would like you to manage the money."

The author asked Audrey who was the executor of her father's will. Audrey said that it was her stepmother.

The author asked Audrey about her financial situation beyond the inheritance. As Audrey shared her personal information, the author found that Audrey had hardly any savings of her own, despite the fact that she was soon to be approaching retirement age. She proudly told the story of how she grew up in France in a magnificent house with the privilege, prestige and the niceties that wealth provides.

With great excitement, Audrey flew to her homeland, but finding her situation differently than she expected. Audrey learned that there was no money left for her to inherit. She still does not know what happened to her inheritance, but the money was completely gone. Audrey never found her stepmother or her children.

The fortune Audrey believed as her retirement never came into her possession. Obviously (and sadly) she no longer needed the author to manage her imaginary wealth.

AUTHOR'S NOTES

It is a tragedy that Audrey was expecting an inheritance, especially such a large sum, and learned one day that there was nothing left for her. But who was to blame? No one. Unless you are the executor of the most recent will of the decedent, there is no guarantee that you will receive an inheritance. As long as people are of legal age and have a sound mind, they can always change their wills to a new one, and the previous will becomes null and void.

A greater tragedy is that Audrey saved almost nothing for her retirement since she was counting on her inheritance. If she were younger, she could have had the time to save, but it's hard to save up when you are almost at retirement age.

Unless you are ABSOLUTELY sure of getting a large inheritance, it is prudent to save your own money.

WISDOM FROM THE EXPERTS AND PROFESSIONALS

Linda Klein, *former President of the American Bar Association, the first woman president of the State Bar of Georgia, and senior managing shareholder at the Baker Donelson law firm.*

Retirement looks different for everyone, depending on what businesses people are in, what their life situations are like, and the problems and issues they are facing. In good times or in specialized industries, some business owners cannot find enough qualified labor and have trouble planning for growth. That requires them to think about how to make themselves the best employers they can be. They have to come up with benefit plans for their employees that make the job sticky so that people want to stay.

In tougher economic times, business owners have to be careful not to grow too fast for fear of spending too much revenue. Depending on the industry, it might be a good time to take advantage of a strong pool of talent to upgrade.

Some of my clients are facing changes as they approach retirement. They don't want to work as hard anymore. They've worked for forty or fifty years, and now they're ready to sell their business or just close it down. Sometimes, in selling a business, particularly a professional practice, you have to keep working. You're used to owning the business and suddenly you're working for the person you're selling it to, which is just not as exciting. You may even disagree with the new management. You want to run the business the way you've always ran it, but then again, you don't own it anymore. A growing group of people have just decided to close the door if they can't find someone who'll buy it outright so that they can retire from the business or move on to something else.

Sending children to college is obviously a pressing issue for anybody with children because the cost of a college education has so far exceeded inflation that people who started planning for it have found that no matter how hard they try, they can never put away enough money for college. But for people who are past that very pressing issue, some are worried about whether their parents will run out of money. People are living longer and they're not as healthy in the final years of their lives and they need care. Very few people have long-term care insurance. Some people who have money when they're younger, have been smart enough to put away a chunk of their money and agreed not to touch it. In saving, they are self-insuring for long-term care.

According to AARP, most people in middle age are worried that they will have memory problems. That's the number one issue that concerns people. Many people are concerned about how they're going to take care of themselves. Many are also trying to take care of parents who have those issues already. A pressing financial issue is planning for being sick or needing long-term care. The fear of running out of money with people living longer is very real.

People who can't sleep at night because of financial issues probably have done a poor job of planning. They find themselves in a position where they can't do what they want to do at this stage of their life. The best advice you can give to anyone, particularly a young person, is that the sooner you start planning financially for your future and saving money, the better. I've seen a lot of people who get "house poor," meaning that their mortgage payment is too big a percentage of their income, and they can't put anything into savings. They can't save for their own future. They can't save for their children's college, and they wind up putting it off to the point that it becomes too late. The way to avoid staying up at night when you're in middle age, is to think about savings and planning when you're young. If you are the parent of children who are finishing their education and starting their careers, one of the most important gifts you can give them is the gift of a financial planner who can help them make good choices and good decisions when they're young.

It's important to me to tell people about compounding and what that means. When people are thinking about retirement, they also have to think about their estate plan. When they do that, they need to think about what happens at different stages of life. When your children are young, think about their guardians and having enough resources so that they could live comfortably if you were gone. As you get older, think about whether your children need money or what charities are important to you. Parenting a child with special needs probably keeps you up at night because, even if you can provide for that child financially into their adulthood, you worry about who will take care of your child's needs if you're gone and making sure that they're not taken advantage of by others. I once had a client who had a child with special needs. These people were in their late eighties and their child was in his fifties. He couldn't take care of himself. They unfortunately thought that it was a good idea to get him married off to someone who would take care of him. That, as you can imagine, ended in a disaster. They worried about their son until the day they died.

Erica Dumpel, *Medicare Counselor and Founder at Czajkowski, Dumpel, & Associates, Inc.*

I consult with many people who are coming into the Medicare system. The biggest thing I see is that people have a tremendous fear of making a mistake. The Medicare enrollment is unnecessarily complex, and the government really does not allow you any do-overs. The decision-making pressure makes people almost terrified.

The biggest fear people have is the penalty for late enrollment. If people don't enroll in a timely manner, they could have a 12-month penalty. Many people can face a lifetime penalty. The biggest penalty is for not enrolling punctually. In that case an individual would not have qualifying coverage, and could be prevented from enrolling in Medicare until the first quarter of the following year. That enrollment between January first and the end of March would produce an effective date of July first. Imagine the poor person who discovers they have a problem in April. It will be well over a year before they can get onto Medicare. They cannot get individual coverage through the Affordable Care Act because they're Medicare eligible. That's a terror for a lot of people.

The second big concern is the cost of premiums versus the cost of care. Do I have to enroll in Medicare? Should I stay on my group medical plan? How big is my group? If my group is more than twenty employees, then I don't really have to do anything, but should I enroll in Medicare A? Will I be automatically enrolled if I'm receiving Social Security payments? Can it happen automatically whether I need the coverage or not? If I'm with a group of less than 20 employees, what happens if I don't enroll in Medicare A and B? What if I choose an individual Medicare option? Do I need a Medicare supplement? Do I get Medicare Advantage? Which drug plan is going to have my prescriptions? What in the world! There are so many opportunities for making mistakes! What would be the worst mistake, paying premiums for a plan with low out of pocket expenses or not paying premiums, but facing $6,000 to $8,000 in expenses when something goes wrong?

The third Medicare issue is one that I encourage all financial advisors to get involved with: identifying if an individual was a high earner 2 years ago. If an individual's modified adjusted gross income was above $170,000 2 years earlier then that person's Medicare part B premium will likely go above the $144.60/month base rate. Had that person worked with his or her financial advisor prior to enrolling in Medicare, premiums could possibly have been controlled. Would there have been a good opportunity to do some income planning with a financial advisor, either deferred compensation or restructuring investments so that they are less dividend driven, less capital gains driven—is there a way? If it's not possible to get below the $170,000, they could at least get below the other thresholds? So between CPAs and the financial advisors, all of those folks need to be aware where those thresholds are and that they do move every year. And as we do in tax planning, a couple of dollars will get you into a lower tax bracket where you have the opportunity to reduce premiums as much as possible.

Making the best long-term decision keeps many people up at night. If I make a bad decision in my forties and I suddenly have a large financial responsibility, I can get a second job to pay this thing off. When I'm sixty-five, seventy or older, if I make a bad decision and I'm on a fixed income, whether it is a pension plan or a retirement plan, I can no longer just jump out and make some quick money. These are the kinds of things that concern people. If I make a bad decision, it is more difficult to get over it and to get beyond it.

One of my favorite stories that I often share is not about a person who made a mistake, it was Medicare that made the mistake. We had an employee at a firm who was sent to us. His wife had an end-stage renal disease. When someone is disabled as a result of disability and qualifies for Social Security disability in the 25th month of receiving that income, that individual qualifies for Medicare. However, end stage renal disease is a little bit different. It is a day one qualifier. The day someone receives that diagnosis, they qualify for Medicare. Understanding this, the family called Medicare. They were told "No, you can't qualify for Medicare now. You have to wait." That's when they came to me. I asked them to call

Medicare again and ask for a supervisor. They were given the same answer. I told the family, "I know that's not right. It says so right here on the Medicare website." We realized that this was not a state issue. Going to the state's insurance commissioner wouldn't help us. This was a federal issue. We called a congressman. We found a staff support person in the congressman's office who could help. This poor family had had several months of trauma trying to figure out how to resolve this issue, but after calling the congressman, the issue was resolved in twenty minutes.

Another favorite story is about a firm I visited in North Georgia. They had fewer than twenty employees. When I got there, I discovered that three of the employees were over age 65 and did not have Medicare A and B. I had to tell the owner he couldn't do that. The insurance company reserves the right not to pay claims that Medicare is responsible for. But the owner said, "No, we're paying our premiums." I told him, "Well, good luck. You really don't want to be the person who's holding the bag when there's a big claim and the insurance company says that they are not responsible." The owner agreed to make some changes and we were able to get Medicare. This was a blessing because within the next couple of months, two of the employees retired and they would not have qualified for Medicare at that time had we not gotten them enrolled. This was a wonderful long-term positive for those employees. It was very good for the employer, too. Imagine if something had happened to those employees and this had blown up in a small town in North Georgia. A whole lot of bad press was avoided by doing the right thing.

Most mistakes happen by not planning. Many people make these decisions by doing what their neighbor, their friend, their family member has done. Not everybody wears a size ten red cleat or a size six red pump. The same thing is true for retirement planning. People don't tend to plan in advance, whether they're selling a business, retiring, or getting divorced. These are not overnight decisions. If we can start encouraging CPAs and financial advisors and employers to start talking to employees four or five years before retirement, I think everybody would make better decisions. Because if someone is getting divorced and the spouse who is employed is made responsible for the former spouse's coverage, the attorneys and the judge can decide whatever they want, but the insurance company is not necessarily going to follow suit. So plan ahead. The same is true for those with high income. Is there a way to create a deferred compensation plan or restructure income? Plan and get ahead of that. Be aware of the possible issues you may come up against planning for your retirement. This should not be a surprise. It's all written out there. We just need to be aware of it.

Susan Brown, *Senior Market Specialist from Multiplied Benefits Architecture*

Understanding what Medicare Parts A, B, C, and D is a big challenge for people getting into Medicare. How do they all work together, what is the difference between them, and which one does a person need? It will be different for each person. The basic program of Medicare, the piece that every single Medicare enrollee needs is Medicare part A, part B, and a prescription drug plan, which is part D. The supplement and the Medicare part C or the Medicare Advantage plans are optional that is their choice to make for additional coverage. But Medicare Part A, B, and D are the basics. Everyone needs to have that as minimum.

There is a lot of confusion about the terminologies on

Medigap, Supplement, Medicare Part C, and Advantage. People use terminology in a wrong way. They do not know the difference between the two. Medigap and Supplement are two terms used to describe the same product. And Medicare part C and Medicare Advantage are two terms used to describe the same product. Using the correct terminology and educating someone about what they are supposed to say will help distinguish between those two programs. But they are two different types of Medicare programs. It's important to know that Medicare whether you are getting those benefits through the federal program of A and B and choosing not to purchase anything else to go with it or if you are choosing to purchase the Supplement Plan to go with your Medicare A and B or if you are choosing to the Advantage program to go with your Medicare A and B. All three of those options are providing the same amount of benefit. It's all covering the same things, it's going to provide you hospital coverage, doctor coverage, lab and diagnostic tests, doctor visits, and procedures. The distinction is how much it is going to cost you out-of-pocket.

The Medicare Advantage plan, which is Medicare part C, has little to no monthly premium cost to the enrollee. However, when they go see their doctor or they go have a test or they need to be in a hospital, that is when they are going to have to pay. It is a relationship between insurance carrier and the enrollee to cover those claims. The insurance carrier is going to pay a portion and the enrollee is going to pay a portion of those medical claims. On the supplement plans, the enrollee is going to pay a higher monthly plan premium and in exchange for that higher plan premium, they are going to reduce or eliminate their out-of-pocket cost when they need to go see the doctor, have a test or procedure done, or be in the hospital. Supplement plans are designed to cover what

Medicare would otherwise charge. Some people will say they're pretty healthy, they really don't have any medical concerns and don't want to pay a high monthly premium for coverage they're not using on a regular basis. Those people would be more inclined to have a Medicare Advantage plan, because there is not any cost they are incurring above the cost of Medicare itself. But, when something happens, they get sick, injured, or get a check-up with the doctors, that's when they will incur some of those costs.

Medicare part D is the prescription drug coverage program. If a person does not have creditable coverage for prescription drugs, it might be because they chose not to take it or they thought that they had creditable drug coverage and it turned out not to be so. There is a late enrollment penalty for Medicare part D. That penalty amount is 1% of the national average of premium. Every year Medicare releases what their national average of premium is for a prescription drug plan and the penalty is based off of that. It will be 1% penalty for every month the person has been without coverage and should have had coverage. If a person should have had prescription drug coverage at age sixty-five, and at age seventy they discover that they did not have creditable coverage then they will be charged for five years of penalties. Some people actively choose not to take prescription drug coverage and take the penalty. They often make that decision because they are not taking prescription medication daily and say, "I can wait five years and see if my situation changes. If that happens and the penalty comes, then I might have a $15 or $20 per month penalty, but I didn't have to pay five years for a policy that I didn't need."

Often, people who retire at age sixty-five decide to take COBRA because most people understand that to be a continuation of the insurance program they had with their employer. They decide they can do that for 18 months. What they don't understand is that Medicare does not consider COBRA as a creditable coverage, because they are not actively employed. The only way to delay Medicare without penalty is with active employment. Concerning Medicare, if you were on COBRA prior to age sixty-five and become Medicare eligible, your COBRA will end when you elect Medicare. If someone makes the mistake and continues on COBRA beyond age 65 without electing Medicare, there is a penalty. They will be penalized financially in how much premium they will be charged to come into Medicare at a later date. There could also be some claims coverage issues. COBRA is a secondary insurance, not a primary insurance like Medicare. If somebody finds that they need to be hospitalized or have a major surgery and they have COBRA, they may be responsible for a very large portion of that claim.

Your insurance coverage should be reviewed every year. That is not necessary when you have a Supplement plan, but it is a very important practice when you have a Medicare Advantage plan or a prescription drug plan, which is Part D. The cost of those plans changes annually. If you just enroll, set it aside, and forget about it, you might find out that a medication that was covered is no longer covered and you won't have an opportunity to do anything about it for a year. Or, you might find out that your doctor, or a facility that they are using under that plan, a hospital system, a diagnostic center for diabetes or chemotherapy or things of that nature no longer take that plan.

It's great to speak with your friends and family to get an understanding of what their plans look like, what kind of cost they are incurring, but you shouldn't take recommendations from them based on what they did, because your needs and health could be different than theirs. You really need to make sure you are selecting a plan that is not only meeting your needs today, but will help you in the future. A person may be very healthy right now and may not have any medical concerns, but ten years from now if they get a medical diagnosis like cancer, they are going to be more inclined to seek the best care possible. Depending on what they selected at the beginning of their retirement, there may be limitations. Insurance is a very big decision, and it is intended to be a permanent decision, which is why we want to look towards the future.

Heather Schreiber, RICP® *Founder and President at HLS Retirement Consulting, LLC*

When people start to think about their Social Security benefits, they have three common concerns. The first concern is that Social Security won't be there for them in the future. The second is that they don't have enough information to make an informed decision, and the third concern is that they don't know where to get it. Every year, the Social Security board of trustees puts out a report of the status of the OASDI trust funds, which is essentially funded by Social Security and Medicare. If no changes are made to the Social Security laws, it is estimated that there will be enough in the trust funds to pay 80% of promise to benefits through 2035. The question I get particularly from people approaching retirement is whether this situation would affect them. My best guess is that folks in their mid-to late- fifties don't have anything to worry about. Younger folks will be affected, but there's a lot of time for Social Security rules to be changed. Changes might include increasing the taxable wage base or increasing the age for full retirement. Right now, the latest full retirement age for those born in 1960 or later is age 67, but that could change as life expectancy increases. My thought: don't let that be the compelling reason to run to the Social Security office and file for benefits.

I often hear people say, "I don't understand this enough to know what I don't know." Meaning, what do I need to consider? That is a concern and certainly http://socialsecurity.gov is a great place to start navigating the factors that go into a claim. Aligning yourself with a trusted advisor is helpful as well because the Social Security administration is not able to provide advice on filing. Therefore, it's really important to empower yourself. Since 90% of Americans will collect Social Security in some form or fashion, it is important to consider the entire scenario thoughtfully and make a wise decision. For most people, that is the only guaranteed source of income they'll have in retirement, so it's an important decision to make.

I work with financial advisors for their client's Social Security. One advisor had a couple who were both turning sixty. The husband had been in the workforce for his entire career and had made substantial earnings. His retirement benefit at full retirement age was about $3,000 per month. His wife had been in and out of the workforce because she raised their family. Her benefit was much smaller, about a $1,000 per month. They planned to file for Social Security at sixty-two. The reason he wanted to file so early was because, historically, none of the men in his family lived beyond the age of seventy-five. In his mind, filing early made sense so that he could get more years of benefit. If it were just him, that probably would have been a really good decision, mathematically. But when I ran an analysis, assuming he passed away at seventy-five and only giving her an average life expectancy of eighty-seven, it still made better sense for him to wait until seventy before filing. The reason for waiting was because his wife would then inherit a much higher survivor benefit upon his death. If he did only live to age seventy-five, she would receive a higher survivor benefit much sooner than a couple who had relatively average life expectancies. A lot of people don't quite understand the effect of the higher wage earners claiming decision on their lower earnings. When one spouse passes, the smaller benefit goes away. For him to file at sixty-two versus seventy made a substantial difference in her monthly income after he passed away.

One of the most often missed opportunities to leverage benefits to increase income during retirement is with widows and widowers. Let's suppose that a widow, whose spouse recently passed away, hasn't yet taken a Social Security benefit for her own retirement or the survivor benefit. At the time of her spouse's death she is sixty-three. When she goes to the Social Security office, she will likely be told to file for both benefits simultaneously. Then she will receive the higher of the two benefits for the rest of her life. What the office typically doesn't share, is that she could take the smaller benefit first and then switch over to the higher benefit later. For example: let's assume that the survivor benefit is $2,000 a month. And then let's suppose that the surviving spouse's benefit is also $2,000 a month. If the surviving spouse would collect the reduced survivor benefit at age sixty-three, it would be slightly reduced because she would be claiming it before her full retirement age. However, she could take the survivor benefit now and then tell Social Security office to hold off on giving her, her own benefit so that she's earning 8% per year every year until she turns seventy. This is one of the most often missed opportunity by widows and widowers.

Joanne Max, *PhD., Clinical Psychologist, Clinical Neuropsychologist, College Planning Consultant*

For women who are retiring, a big issue many of them face is a loss of identity, a loss of community, and feelings of isolation. They have lost a part of who they are and must make an entire life change because they're no longer working. The older adults that I see: women who have retired either by choice or they have been forced into retirement, or who have divorced or become widows, struggle with grief, loss, fear, depression, and anxiety. They also struggle with security and stability. If they haven't handled the family finances, they are now thrown into a situation that's unfamiliar and they're having to try to manage all of that while simultaneously grieving the loss of their spouse. I see women in many transitions: women who are married or single parents who are trying to plan for their children's education and college struggle with being realistic about their financial situation, perhaps regretting that they hadn't looked at it earlier and managed their financial planning better and feel guilt or shame as a result and struggle with setting financial limits with their children in college planning.

Clients typically come in with very distorted thoughts about themselves. They have a lot of negative perceptions and beliefs. They're depressed, frightened, anxious, and very self-critical. They think they're stupid, that they don't know how to handle any of these things, and that they're worthless. I work to challenge those distorted thoughts and negative beliefs. I like to call it "stinking thinking" and I help empower them to look at what they can do. I turn them to the support services and resources that can help them resolve their problems and work through these difficulties; I empower them to take control of their personal lives, their financial lives, and their emotional lives.

Many face anxiety and depression because of their lack of financial stability: security, cash flow, medical expenses, debts, and loans. Many worry about outliving their finances or being able to pay their bills, which leads to a lot of trouble sleeping, feelings of insecurity, regret, and self-critical rumination at night. I call it "motor mind at night," when your mind races, making it hard to think and concentrate during the day. They feel like a failure when they've lost financial support.

I've worked with several older adults who thought their life was fairly stable and comfortable, when all of a sudden they lose a job or have unexpected health problems and have to stop working. One woman was divorced and had financial management challenges, and then got out of another relationship that had significant financial problems. In these cases, the women were in their seventies and had to go back to work and having to find a position in their seventies was not an easy task. These changes in circumstances lead to very different identities and a sense of loss of competence.

One couple I worked with was financially secure until disaster hit. The one spouse was a successful professional and the other spouse stayed home and ran the household and took care of the children. Then the professional had a stroke. Unfortunately, the area of the brain in which the stroke occurred, affected his judgment. This led to a cascade of financial decisions that were terrible for the family. The spouse spent money recklessly and made terrible decisions, accumulating massive expenses such as wanting to make renovations with the house and buying another house—devastating financial decisions. This family had children in private school and some were in college. The wife had no credit herself and had no access to the funds. It was all in her husband's name. Everything was online and she had no ability to access the accounts or open an account in her name and transfer money from her husband's accounts. It was frightening to watch a person with a true medical problem, but who wasn't declared incompetent, cause so much devastation. They couldn't legally stop the bad financial decisions that were wiping away the family finances. The wife was unable to interrupt the waste, open other accounts, or share in managing paying bills.

If she had, at the very least, had shared access to the accounts, had her name on the account, had access to the credit cards, the places where loans were being taken out, they would have been able to handle things far better and felt much more able to stop the landslide of finances going out the window.

Rhoda Margolis, *LCSW, Atlanta Chapter Co-Founder at The Transition Network*

We are a group for women age fifty and forward. Some are retired, some are working full time but thinking ahead toward retirement, and some are working part time. These women have many varied concerns but one of the main issues is health. When you're young, you don't think about how your health impacts your life. I have also noticed that many women are just not interested in finances. They don't want to think about it, and they are in denial. We just had a wonderful speaker come in to our office who talked about money and finances. We needed to have at least ten people to participate. We didn't get ten people. While many women are frightened of money issues, they won't participate in a meeting like this.

It is a big issue. How do you know that you're not going to outlive your funds? What do you do then? It's important to plan for the future and to think about these things.

The workplace gives you a lot more than just a salary. You have relationships with your co-workers, you have structure to your day and your week. You feel like you're contributing to your community. You give all that up, in a sense, when you retire, and you need to find ways to apply yourself. They say social relationships are one of the five key things for a healthy person. You get that in the workplace if you work in a healthy work setting. But how are you going to get that when you're not in the workplace? That's another key concern.

Some of our younger retirees have elderly parents or siblings and have to take long-term caregiving into consideration. It's not unusual for a seventy-year-old to have a ninety-five-year-old parent. That presents a whole lot of other concerns that people are dealing with at this point in life. I met someone whose mother would call her twenty times a day. Then the mother would fall in the middle of the night and she would have to go over to help her. It can be very difficult. Long-term care issues are related to that. If you don't start saving for your retirement when you're in your thirties, you're going to be behind the eight ball. I don't know anybody in their thirties who is thinking about retirement. They are paying off school loans, buying a house, raising kids, and paying for the kids' college tuitions. It's daunting and costly.

It's easy to make a mistake in planning because it's very complicated. I know someone who took her Social Security early at sixty-two, but what she didn't realize was that when she turned sixty-five, she wouldn't make up for anything. She would always get her Social Security based on the amount she started with at age sixty-two. If she had known, she would have planned very differently. By the time she found that out, it was too late. It's very complicated. When my husband and I were ready to get Medicare, we were fortunate that somebody recommended a gentleman who came and met with us and spoke to us about every plan. He brought a long list of what each plan offered, helping us figure out what the best plan was going to be for us. If you don't even know that that kind of person exists, you might make the wrong choice. So when you're getting older, you have so much to think about in regards to retirement.

Retirement is wonderful for me. I retired in 2011. I'm fortunate to be able to be enjoying my retirement. I loved my work and I miss it, but I wanted my time. I wanted to be free of the demands of other people. You don't know how much longer you will live. It could be a day. It could be twenty years. I worked for 42 years. You go to school, you graduate, you get a job, you get married, you have children, you're working, it's a lot of time dedicated to other people. I felt like it was time for me to leave work. I miss it in a way—not that I want to go back to it, but I do miss my colleagues. I do some volunteering and I still go in and meet friends for lunch. I'm a clinical social worker. I've worked as a therapist and a supervisor. I helped the agency grow significantly and was very involved in the community. I'm very satisfied with my accomplishment.

Forced Retirement

Jonathan Ginsberg, *Social Security Disability Attorney and Owner at Ginsberg Law Offices*

One of the concerns that many people have is developing a medical problem and they can no longer work. Due to the medical issue, at some point, they're either terminated from their job or they begin to get negative reviews at work. They get to the point where they can simply no longer work and they don't know what to do. If they don't have any other source of income or private long-term disability insurance, they could then file for Social Security disability. A lot of people don't know that Social Security disability exists. Many people are aware of Social Security retirement, but there is an entire disability program for folks who do not have the capacity to work anymore, unlike retirement, which is based on age and is automatic. With disability, however, you must prove that you have a long-term medical condition that prevents you from working. That condition must be something that has lasted or is expected to last a year or more.

Social Security Disability is not a very efficient system. It can take two to three years from the time somebody applies to the time benefits are approved. The benefit adjudication process is somewhat arbitrary in that a person with two identical claimants might have different results depending on the judges who are assigned to them. It can be quite a wide range. That can be very frustrating. When someone is no longer able to work, that creates not only financial problems, but also interpersonal issues. They lose socialization associated with work. Their family can be stressors. They may have family members or relatives who don't understand the problem and say, "You look fine, why aren't you working?" Downsizing from two incomes to one can lead to a lot of family stress and domestic problems. It can be very depressing. A lot of people develop what I would call situational depression because they go from being productive and making a good living to sitting at home, not knowing what's going on, and not having a lot of hope.

When people start to have health problems that could

lead to this kind of situation, I often find that many people don't change their lifestyle immediately. If they start cutting back their expenses to only the things they need, they could lower the charges to their credit cards. But since many people don't cut back and keep the same expenses, their credit card debts pile up very quickly as soon as they are no longer able to bring income to the households.

Disability insurance will give relief in financial problems. There are basically two categories of disability insurance: company (group) provided and individual provided. In my practice, I would say no more than about 10% of people have either one of those.

It is important to keep a frugal lifestyle. Spend within what you bring home and try to minimize your debts.

Heather K. Karrh, *Partner at Rogers, Hofrichter & Karrh, LLC*

I represent people who lose their primary source of income due to disability and whose disability insurance policy is all they have left. It was part of their economic plan to survive bad events. But then they find out that the insurance company is not paying them the benefits. So not only are they disabled, they've lost their job, and their insurance policy isn't paying. Most of my clients do have some money beyond their disability insurance, but it doesn't last very long. By the time they come to me, they've already cashed out their 401(k). It's rough.

The benefits they are eligible for depend on the policy. If they have a group policy through work, an ERISA governed policy, then the average amount is anywhere from 60% to 66% of their basic monthly earnings. Sometimes they can buy up and get a little bit more, but usually that will only increase to the 70% range. If they have purchased private insurance, then they can get more coverage.

In terms of the claims, a carrier for an individual policy will usually pay, depending on the carrier and their clauses. I would say that the individual policies are generally written more favorably—as in everything, you get what you pay for. If you pay more, you're going to get a better policy. I'm not supposed to give tax advice, but it is a good idea to pay for the premiums with after tax dollars. If you do that, it is a tax-free benefit and that can save you a good deal of money when you receive the monthly disability benefits.

When my clients submit their claims, they don't usually make a mistake per se, but they don't send in enough information to the insurance company. It is their burden to prove disability. People don't realize that, so they will apply to the insurance company and give only their doctors' names and addresses. They don't actually send the medical records, which is important to do. In order to win the lawsuit and get your claim paid, you need three things: a good doctor who's in your corner and willing to support you, an objective medical illness (it is always much easier if it's something that can be proven objectively proven), and you need a decent lawyer.

The sooner you can get to a lawyer, the better it is. There are many legal hurdles that many people don't realize. One of them is simply sending in your medical records and your prescription records, which are very important because medical records are not always detailed but prescription records show more.

Most of my cases are people whose claims have been rejected by their insurance company. One of my clients was on disability insurance. His doctor was out of the office one day and the insurance companies sent some forms over. Another doctor, who had never seen my client and knew nothing about the case, filled out the forms and said that he could work. That took a while to get straightened out. Eventually the judge ruled it as a mistake. It had to go all the way to litigation to straighten out the issue, even though it was clearly a mistake by a doctor who hadn't seen the patient.

I represented an emergency room doctor who had a mental illness that meant she could no longer perform as an emergency room doctor. She also ran a business. The insurance company looked at her case and said, "Well, she only worked in the emergency room part time. She could still work in her business, so she wasn't totally disabled." That's a pretty common argument. The insurance company will concede that you can't do one thing, but then they'll say that your occupation is another. The carrier argued that the doctor's occupation was running the business. For her, it would have been better to have practice specific language and she did not really have that.

The other thing that they commonly argue is contestability. The preexisting condition clauses, by law, can only be contested in Georgia for up to two years maximum. For most policies it's one year, and that's not very long. Contested cases can take up to five years. For example, in cases of depression, insurance companies will try to contest the policy based on the individual having been depressed in college. They say, "When you filled out the form, you didn't tell us that you were depressed in college." Well, everybody gets a little depressed in college. You have to be careful.

Mental illness is one of the main issues that cause carriers to reject their payments. If someone becomes disabled due to mental illness, there's a limitation. It's a huge debate and the 11th circuit court has some good case law on mental limitations. Basically, there is a way to get around a mental limitation. Mental limitations are fairly common, and these policies will only pay up to one or two years for a disorder based on mental illness. Insurance companies do that because mental illnesses are not as objective as other illnesses. Certain mental illnesses are short term, like situational depression from the death of a family member. You're depressed, but you can't know whether or not you're going to be totally disabled from that depression in three years. That's another matter. The insurance company has sound reasons for putting limitations in the policies, however, they do try and take advantage of those quite often.

Causes of mental illness are an issue the insurance company looks at as a sort of loophole: is it a preexisting condition, is it a symptom of another physical ailment, such as Multiple Sclerosis? My advice is to talk to your doctors and establish a good relationship with them. Your doctor is going to be put under a lot of pressure from the insurance companies. The phone calls and the forms they will be asked to fill out by the insurance company take a lot of time and effort. The doctor is not being reimbursed for this usually, or they're being reimbursed very poorly. There are certain doctors, usually veteran's administration doctors and doctors with HMOs, who simply won't fill out disability forms as a rule. Considering all the extra time, you can't blame them. Establish a good relationship with your doctors. And in general, because disability and insurance are tricky, I would say try and get a lawyer involved as early as possible.

CHAPTER **THREE** SUMMARY

1. Find something meaningful to do in your retirement, whether it's a part-time job or volunteering.

2. Start five to ten years before your retirement to find "it" and hone your skills.

3. In the age of living longer, the sooner you start planning and saving for retirement, the better. Instead of saving left over money, save first and figure how to live with the rest of the money.

4. Unless you are absolutely certain, don't count on your inheritance for your retirement. Save your OWN money.

5. Give a gift of a financial planner to your kids when they start working.

6. Do Medicare planning before age sixty-five. This could lead to lower Medicare costs.

7. If you are working for a firm with twenty or fewer workers, file for Medicare at sixty-five even though you plan to work longer.

8. See your financial advisor before you start taking Social Security benefits at sixty-two.

9. If you become a widow, don't forget to check into your survivor benefits.

10. Get involved in your family's finances; don't let your spouse handle them all.

11. Get involved in a support group for retirees. This may make your transition to retirement smoother.

12. Plan for the possibility of forced retirement through disability.

What's Your Money Story? Find out: **www.ChooseYourMoneyStory.com**

CHAPTER FOUR

Widowhood

*"Weeping may endure for a night, but
joy cometh in the morning."*

—PSALMS 30:5

THE WORD *WIDOW* sounds like it is referring to "old" ladies. However, the average age of widowhood is just 59 years old.[1] Many widows may live several decades after the death of their spouses. According to the Financial Transitionist Institute (FTI), from which I earned my Certified Financial Transitionist® (CeFT) designation, 80% of men die while still married, where 80% of women die single.

At FTI, we say that transitions have three or four stages: Anticipation (this is not necessary in unanticipated events), Ending, Passage, and New Normal. I mentioned *Four Stages of Transition* at the very beginning of this book which you can use for any change in your life. In this chapter, let's apply the *Four Stages of Transition* for Widowhood.

---

1. U.S. Census Bureau

Four Stages of Transition

From what was
to what will be

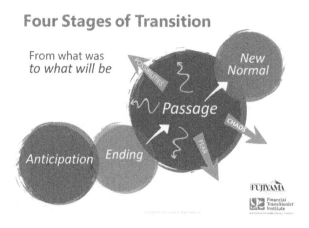

STAGE 1: *Anticipation*, is when you expect something might happen to your spouse. At this stage, you might feel hopeless and/or start thinking about your life without your spouse in the near future.

STAGE 2: *Ending* is when death happens. Your finances haven't necessarily shifted, but there is no going back from the reality of the death. During this stage, you might get overwhelmed and/or confused. As a result, you might have difficulty with follow through.

STAGE 3: In the *Passage* stage you have transferred your spouse's money and the checklist of transfers are done. However, you might not feel grounded or settled. Instead, you might feel depleted, exhausted, unable to function well cognitively, emotionally, at work, or in other important areas. You feel loss of identity. Of the four stages, *passage* by far takes the longest, usually years.

STAGE 4: During the *New Normal* stage, you find you can speak about your spouse's death in past tense and are able to look back and see how things came together. You have a sense of relief and energy. You are able to do long-term and short-term thinking and planning. FTI's founder, Susan Bradley, CFP®, CeFT® says, "When money changes, life changes, and when life changes, money changes."

Let's learn from the participants from this chapter and minimize the "*money change*" during this sad event that could happen in our lives.

SARAH'S STORY:
No Identity After Fifty Years

A successful Atlanta entrepreneur, Jay, tells the story of his mother, Sarah. She went to Oglethorpe University in the 1930s and became a podiatrist. She went to college because her grandfather told her that just by sitting in classes, she would learn something. She was a bit of a difficult child in terms of school and education, but she was a go-getter who could sell and do anything she put her mind to. The family had a successful business and a good name in Atlanta. She drove the success of the business.

After my father passed away, Jay says, my mother went to get a credit card since she realized that she had been using his credit card for the past fifty years. She was rejected because she'd never had a credit card in her own name. Jay's advice to any woman who is married, is to get a credit card in your own name, just in case, God forbid, something happens. "That's the advice I think my mother would like to give to people, especially to women."

AUTHOR'S NOTES

It doesn't matter how successful you are if you don't have credit in your own name. Pay bills with your own credit card and start building up your credit score if you don't have one. Financial institutions only look at what you have under your name, not your intangible reputation.

CINDY'S STORY:

If I Had Worked with a Financial Advisor Earlier, . . .

I fell in love and got married young, at the age of nineteen, and I had my first child when I was twenty. I was very happily married; Parker was my first love and we quickly had three children. I was a stay-at-home mom and he was in sales. We really had the textbook life. We had the two story house with the wraparound porch and the picket fence, and we went to church every Sunday. When I was twenty-nine, and the kids were nine, seven and four, Parker unexpectedly died.

Parker took care of all the finances. He paid the bills and I got an allowance. I didn't really even have a checkbook. I didn't know anything about money, and I never had a job either. So not only was I trying to deal with the kids, but I was trying to get my head around what I would do financially and where I would get a job and earn money because now I didn't have a paycheck coming in.

Parker had a life insurance policy for $50,000 that his parents had taken out when he was young. I was able to continue paying the mortgage from the life insurance proceeds. We lived in Tennessee and the cost of living there was cheap. The children received survivor benefits from his death, which was probably around $2,000 a month and that helped a lot. I found a job, too. We weren't living high on the hog, by any stretch of the imagination, but we weren't going hungry and we made it work. We didn't go out to eat or live extravagantly and we were okay.

This was in the 90s, when everything was deregulating. My first job was in telemarketing. Nowadays everybody hates telemarketing, but back in those days, it didn't have the same stigma. I worked for Sprint calling people. Anybody I got on the phone, I could sell them something. I quickly became the best salesperson there. I guess I had some natural selling ability. After a couple months of that, the leadership team, our managers, found out that I could use a computer. I had a computer at home and had taught myself how to use Word, Excel, and how to build an Access database. I started working in their data-entry department. I learned all about the tariffs; it could sometimes get complex, but I did a pretty good job. I learned quickly, people liked working with me, and the managers liked me, so I ended up becoming a manager.

I was still young at this time, probably 31, and I had no experience managing people. I knew how to get work done, and I was smart, but I couldn't get the girls to come in off their work break. I couldn't get them to care about the quality of their work. I got so frustrated that I'd go talk to my boss in tears and told him that I needed help. His suggestion was for me to write a manual on how to manage people. I went to the library and did the research, but it didn't really help me. What I needed was some coaching. I would come home every day so stressed out. At the same time, my daughter was in fourth grade and she wasn't reading well and I didn't have the time to help her.

So, I marched into my boss's office one morning and said, "I quit." He was like, "Well, you can't quit." And I said, "Yes I can quit. That's what I am doing. I've been telling you how frustrated and unhappy I am for months." He asked me what I was going to do. I said, "I'm going to take the three kids, the two dogs, and the cat, we are going to rent a U-Haul truck, and we're going to Nebraska." This may sound stereotypical and I guess it is, but we were living in East Tennessee and I looked around thinking, I don't want to raise my children here. It's very backwards. There's not a lot of opportunity here and I just couldn't do it. I looked for alternative places to live. I even thought about homesteading in Alaska or New Zealand. I thought about all kinds of crazy things, but those things quickly became way too expensive. I even thought about buying a Winnebago and just driving around to all the State Parks. But then I decided I couldn't live with three kids, two dogs, and a cat in Winnebago.

In Western Nebraska, they had a lot of homesteads. The big farmers would buy all this land and build homes on it. They needed to have people live in the homes because then they got a school tax credit. So, they would rent the homes for practically nothing. I rented a nice home for my family, nothing spectacular: a basic ranch with three bedrooms. We had a barn, a garage, well water, propane gas, and we burned our trash. The best part was it cost $150 a month. I was able to get some goats from an auction and we had chickens. There was a farm up the road from me where I got a job cleaning out chicken coops and horse stalls and filling in prairie dog holes so the horses wouldn't trip. She paid me and taught me about the farm. I even bought a horse from her and she taught me to ride.

I learned a lot since Parker passed away. I didn't even know financial advisors existed for a long time. I had a pretty sheltered life. I was so focused on just meeting our day-to-day needs that it never occurred to me to sit down with somebody and say, "This is how much money I have. This is my monthly budget. Here are my bills. I've got three kids I need to raise and get through college." I knew at that point I was not going to qualify to work with a wealth manager, but I think even then if I had known there was somebody I could reach out to, that could have helped me budget and plan, that would have taken a lot of stress off of me. I worried about money constantly.

Since I didn't talk to an advisor, I never thought about planning for the future. I'm ashamed to say that even after Parker died, I didn't have life insurance. It never occurred to me to get it. What if I had died? What would have happened to my kids? I had no will, I had nothing, and no plan. If I had worked with a financial advisor, I would have been better prepared for the future. I would have been educated on what I could do, instead of lost and knowing nothing about how to move forward.

AUTHOR'S NOTES

It helps your future finances if you find a financial advisor, even at a young age, who is willing to work with you. You will learn from your advisor what you didn't know that you should know. Start early.

Death at a young age sometimes happens. It could happen to you, your spouse, or someone else and only God knows. Risk protection will not wipe out your pain but it could give you relief from your financial burdens.

JAMIE'S STORY:

Life Insurance Kept My Lifestyle

My husband had a sudden heart attack and passed away when our kids were six, nine, and eleven. I had a feeling of absolute shock. Then I went into survival mode for my children's sake. I had no support from my family—none of them lived in this country. They were supportive and tried to help, but, none of our siblings or extended family lived close to me.

I had worked up until my youngest child was born. Then I became a stay-at-home mom. After my husband passed away, I began working part time. One piece of advice that I would share with anybody is to have life insurance. Because you never ever expect something like this to happen to you, especially when you are young and healthy. Thank goodness, we both had life insurance and we had that to fall back on. My husband was only forty years old when he passed away. I've been carrying the load for 13 years.

One of the things that helped during this transition was that I was already managing the family finances before he passed away because he had such a busy work schedule. I was already paying all the bills and running the home primarily on my own. I think that made a huge difference. I knew what everything was and how to do it. That's very important. I think it's crucial in today's world that everybody knows how to handle their own finances because you never know where life is going to take you. You should never be dependent upon somebody else for all of that. It's sad but that's true.

AUTHOR'S NOTES

If you are a stay-at-home mom with kids in a big house and your spouse has a successful job, you may need to take the appropriate amount of life insurance coverage to keep your lifestyle. It's especially true if you don't want to go back to the full time workforce after your spouse's death.

HELEN H'S STORY:
Own Something to Pay You for Life

I met my deceased husband when I was 14 years old. He was a survivor of the Holocaust and an immigrant to this country. He couldn't speak English, but the way he carried himself, I was in love with him like a child with a movie star.

We owned a supermarket and other properties here and there. My husband was a risk taker and went bankrupt three times. It didn't matter to me. He was so positive and wonderful, we had a wonderful life together. He passed away after sixty-two years of marriage.

One thing he did that I am so thankful for is that he sold the supermarket, but he did not sell the ground or the property. He did something called a "Net Net Lease." Whoever leased the property could do whatever they wanted, but they had to pay insurance, taxes, and repairs. As a result, I get the money from the arrangement every month for the rest of my life without needing to manage the building. My husband knew that I was a people person and not for dealing with this stuff. That's everything I have for my retirement on top of the Social Security. But I own this beautiful condo and don't have to worry about paying a mortgage every month which is a big relief for me.

AUTHOR'S NOTES

Helen's husband thought of Helen even beyond his life. That's why she can now live without financial worry.

She is very lucky, but not everyone has the same caring spouse who could plan for her beyond his life. It's important to try to get involved in the family finances from the beginning.

WISDOM FROM THE EXPERTS AND PROFESSIONALS

Ira M. Leff, *Elder Law Attorney at Ira M. Leff Attorney at Law*

The community I serve is primarily made up of people who need long-term care in Georgia. The biggest problem I see is finding a good quality care that is affordable. There are a lot of good assisted living facilities, but Medicaid doesn't subsidize them in Georgia and they typically go for $6,000 to $8,000 a month. Very few families can afford that. A lot of families are forced into placing their loved ones in a nursing home, which is subsidized by Medicaid. Because of the Medicaid system, at least here in Georgia, the quality of care at those facilities and the comfort and pleasantness of those facilities is minimal. Even for those who need to be in nursing homes, sometimes it's difficult to get them in.

I have a case I'm working on right now in which a client was looking at a nursing home in Lawrenceville. When the home found out that my client had a lawyer, they rejected her. They said it was because sometimes it takes lawyers too long to get the people on Medicaid. But I suspect that the real issue is that they get sued a lot and they don't want people coming in who already have a relationship with a lawyer.

I have another case in which a man was in a nursing home and he wasn't happy. He started talking about how he didn't want to live any longer, so they sent him to a mental health hospital. Now we can't get him back into any nursing home because he's considered "high risk." Men in general have a very difficult time getting in because there are fewer male beds in these facilities. Men are oftentimes larger, as far as weight goes, and so it might take two or three staff members to transfer them and therefore it's very difficult to get them placed. Some states have a first come, first serve rule. Georgia, however, does not have that. In Georgia, nursing homes can pick and choose whomever they want in their facility, so they tend to take the most profitable and easy to care for people.

The nursing home lobby in Georgia is extremely strong. The rule is that they're allowed to discriminate on admission. Some states do not allow this. I lobbied against it many years ago and it's just impossible to change anything that the nursing homes want. This is the reason why personal care homes aren't subsidized in Georgia, because the nursing homes have such a strong lobby.

I see a lot of families who go into nursing homes, trusting them to give good advice when it comes to finances. Oftentimes they'll spend a fortune at the nursing home before they go on Medicaid. They could have been eligible for Medicaid long before if they had gotten independent advice instead of expecting or counting on the nursing home to give them fair counsel. I've seen cases in which the nursing home gets an individual on Medicaid when they run out of cash, but they don't tell them that they're going to lose their home when they die because of a state recovery after being in a nursing home. One of the biggest mistakes people make is trusting these facilities to be fair when it comes to legal advice and finances. People trust them because the nursing home administrators seem trustworthy and they don't want to spend money to get good advice—they're already spending the money at the nursing home. Also, they are trusting the nursing home to take care of their loved one, so they assume the nursing home has their best interests in mind. However, nursing homes are in business to make money, and asking them to give you financial advice is ridiculous.

I've had several cases in which people have not gotten advice until their loved one dies. Then they find out about state recovery, which they should have known about from the beginning. Then they want to know how they can keep their property. I have a case now with a family farm. We could have protected the farm easily if the family had asked for legal advice years ago. In this case, the person in the nursing home's son has six kids and one of them is disabled. Medicaid allows gifts to disabled children without limitation. All he had to do was deed the farm to his disabled grandchild during his lifetime and family wouldn't lose it at all when he died. However, nobody at the nursing home gave the family that advice. They didn't care. As long as the nursing home is getting paid by Medicaid, they don't care what happens to the farm or the family. Now I'm fighting with the state recovery department to try to save some of the farm.

Life savings are important to almost everybody. Some people lose sleep over the fact that they think that their kids are going to take their life savings and throw them in a nursing home. Other people are on the other side of the issue, worried that the cost of their long-term care is going to eat into their kids' inheritance; I see both extremes. My job as an elder law attorney is to help my client meet their goal. If their goal is to make sure they don't get thrown into a nursing home, I can set up their assets in such a way that their kids won't have access and they can spend it however they want. If their goal is to make sure that their kids' inheritance is not eaten away, I can help them get into a nursing home and get on Medicaid, preserving the inheritance. The other thing that I see often is older people who could care less about their money. Questions like who's their attorney and who's going to get their money when they die, they could care less about. When we get to the advanced directive, they perk up and they want to talk about it. When it comes to the question of do you want life support, almost all my clients are very strong willed about not being kept alive artificially after they're ready to go.

How they react to the question is different based on their age. I always play devil's advocate when they say they don't want life support. I ask, "Do you trust the doctors, that they know that you're terminally ill? Would you like to try life support for a month or so to see if maybe you'll really come back? Maybe the doctors don't really know." Younger people often times say that they want it, but older people feel like they've already gotten their money's worth, they're in a lot of pain, and life's not so good. They're ready to go when the doctor says it's time to go.

Patricia F. Ammari, *Elder & Special Needs Law Attorney at The Ammari Firm, LLC*

Elderly people have quite a few things that they're concerned about. One is getting their affairs in order; they want to have everything just so to make things easier for their family later. Another concern is the possibility of needing long-term care and the expenses involved in that. I try to help them in different ways. For the more wealthy clients, it's important that they speak with their financial advisor and determine whether or not long-term care insurance would be helpful for them. For folks who have less money and cannot afford long-term care insurance, I typically counsel them regarding the possibility of Medicaid planning and beginning to put systems in place so that if that would ever become necessary, they would be cared for. Long-term care is an ongoing care that's not related to an acute incident, like a broken hip, heart attack, or fall; it's an ongoing condition that will require chronical long-term medical help.

People are often worried about losing everything that they've worked for. If they're married and one of them gets sick, they're concerned about making sure that the other has enough to live on and that they are going to be well taken care of. We try to help them put together a plan so that they can sleep well at night knowing that they've got plans put into place. Sometimes that requires planning with respect to legal documents that allow someone to step in and manage their funds if that becomes necessary.

When they have a child with special needs, they want to make sure that the child is taken care of, too. Oftentimes, when I meet with families in that circumstance, they worry about what would happen if they were not there to take care of their child. That can also be a concern if they have a child who has a drug problem or something else like that. At the end of the day, our most pressing concerns are often our loved ones.

With folks who are not wealthy, I have been hired by the spouse after their loved one who was on Medicaid died. The State then wants to be reimbursed from the loved one's estate. I can offer some help with that, but I could have helped even more if I'd have been involved early on. We could have potentially avoided the situation altogether.

There are others who created their legal documents long ago and don't have a good handle on everything. I'm dealing with a lovely older woman right now whose husband passed away. I was contacted by her CPA because she needs help both with the probating of his estate and with getting everything transferred over to her. She needs a new plan that will help her to be able to go forward, and also planning, possibly through a trust, so that her loved ones can take care of her when the time comes. That's been an ongoing situation of sifting through all the assets, looking at each one and how we need to get them transferred, updating documents, and more. Another experience I am dealing with is with a younger woman who recently lost her husband to cancer. Not only does she need to go through the probate process and get everything switched over into her name, but she needs to put things in place to care for her son, just in case anything happens to her. We're putting a trust in place that will hold assets for her son and take care of him until he reaches an age where he's able to do it himself.

Some transitions I see are for second marriages. Statistically, about half of all marriages end in divorce. Sometimes with the second marriage, the women would like their children to get everything and not their new spouse, who can probably take care of himself. Unless they draw up a new will that actually spells out those terms, that won't be the case and their spouse will automatically get some of their estate.

Estate planning documents, whether a will or a trust, is basically a document that was created for you at that time. But life goes on and changes happen. You should review those plans yourself about every year and just make sure that that is still what you want. Then have an attorney review it maybe every three years or so. Tax laws change and may affect your estate plan and your family circumstances may change as well. A couple of years ago, the state of Georgia changed their power of attorney laws. Everyone should redo their power of attorney plan in order to be able to take advantage of some of the new benefits and the new law. You might not necessarily know about those changes because once you end the relationship with your attorney who drew up the original plans, they're not going to be following up with you.

For folks who are a certain age, I would recommend that when they do their estate planning, that they see not only an estate planning attorney, but also an elder law attorney. The reason for this is that the elder law attorney will be thinking about things that the typical estate planner will not be thinking about. Whether that is dealing with the possibility of having special provisions particularly in the event that someone might need assistance with long-term care (such as Medicaid or VA) or some other event, it's important for there to be certain authority in that power of attorney to cover those things in that trust document.

I've had clients who saw an attorney after they were sick, and who are now struggling with planning for their future. If they had seen an elder law attorney, their issues would have been completely taken care. Now they are stuck with the documents that they had drawn up, which do not allow them to do all the planning that they could have done otherwise. Folks who are dealing with long-term care will save themselves money, headaches, and litigation if they get some advice from an elder care attorney on the front end. It's important to see an attorney and actually get the documents done right to begin with. When you see an attorney, it's not just about the documents. A lawyer brings a lot of benefits to the table that folks might not have even considered.

Laura Jalbert, *LCSW, Licensed Clinical Social Worker and Owner and Clinical Director at Mindful Transitions*

People are living longer now than ever before and the cost of care is higher than what people expect. Many of our patients and their family members are worried that they will outlive their finances. The cost of long-term care is incredibly high and there aren't programs and resources to pay for it. People don't always plan well for long-term care and what they're going to do as they age, get sick, or have medical issues. They may not consider that they have to pay for an aid, somebody to drive them around, prescription costs, and all the expenses that people incur as they get older. Many people do not have long-term care insurance—many people do not know it exists. If they did know of it, it wasn't something that seemed affordable or attainable for them. It's rare when I meet with people who have long-term care policies. Sometimes I've seen folks who have trouble accessing their coverage. They may or may not have met whatever criteria the insurance company requires for their services. Typically, they'll send out a nurse or other professional to meet with the patient. If they don't need enough care, then they don't meet the standard for service.

My clients are often afraid of having to go to a nursing home or having to accept levels of care or changes in care that they don't want. They want to remain in control of their choices, but because of some of the financial challenges that they may have, that's not always possible.

One of the calls that we get fairly often is someone who has purchased inadequate health insurance. They may have multiple chronic medical problems, mental health issues, or a number of conditions combined, and they have purchased a Medicare Advantage plan because that is cost effective. But what they find out when speaking with us is that many of their providers do not accept this coverage, their co-pay, or share of the cost. It is cost prohibitive because of the high copays. Before making a choice about Medicare, they should certainly take a look at whether or not it will cover their current physicians and ultimately what the costs will be if they need to use the insurance. The Medicare Advantage plan could be a great type of plan for someone who doesn't have any medical issues, but not necessarily for someone who needs medical care. If they're the kind of person who would avoid using Medicare because of the costs, they may skip the care that they need in an effort to save money and that could be really dangerous.

One of the things that we try to do is refer our clients in these situations to someone who will review all of their medical conditions and their medications, in conjunction with reviewing their health insurance options, so that they can perhaps make a better choice. Many times it's a matter of paying a little bit more premium on the front end so that you can actually use your coverage as you go, rather than avoiding the care that you need because you can't afford it.

Sometimes we encounter families or situations where an older adult doesn't have insight into what's happening with them anymore. They may be spending more money than they have each month, or making really poor financial decisions, or other medical safety decisions. In those cases, we're working with the adult children to help try and mitigate the risks and keep the older adults safe. Sometimes that requires hospitalization and sometimes the family pursues legal means of guardianship or conservatorship to keep the older adult safe either physically or financially.

If the family members are out of state, it's a little bit more complicated. Oftentimes, we have to refer them to an agency who can be the eyes and ears for them, like someone they can employ with some medical training and medical knowledge to help monitor mom or dad.

Ronnie Genser, *President at Bereavement Navigators*

Many times one of the biggest questions widows who have lost their spouse reflect on is this: "Who will take care of me?" Virtually every time a new widow joined the bereavement support group I attended after the death of my husband, this question was a recurring theme. The issue was not only about having enough money, but also about non-financial issues such as where her physical and emotional support would come from when she had significant health issues and needed to be taken care of, or who would do all the home repairs her husband had done when he was alive?

However, we need to realize widows are really all different and hence, don't have the same emotional and financial needs. They have different concerns and different issues, depending on their age when they become a widow. A widow in her twenties or thirties has different issues than a widow in her fifties and sixties, or even in her seventies or eighties. According to the U.S. Census Bureau, the average age of widowhood in the United States is 59. This surprises most people because it seems so young.

Not knowing how long a widow will live and if she will have enough money to not only meet her daily basic needs, but also to enjoy life, especially given potential inflation issues and the continuing rise of day-to-day expenses, is of special concern for many widows, young and old alike. However, this is especially true for widows who are younger with a longer life expectancy, are healthy, and/or have children at home.

If the widow is older, her major financial concerns are typically compounded not only by concerns about paying for good care as needs arise, be it for home care, adult day care, home healthcare, assisted living, and/or nursing home care, but also for how long she will need care and how much it will cost, especially in today's world when many people are living into their mid-80s and sometimes into their late 90s. The key financial questions then become: how long will my money last and will I have enough for these costly expenses?

In addition, there are many other issues and questions a widow or an adult child on behalf of a parent may face after the death of a spouse or parent. One of my clients, an adult child, engaged me on behalf of her widowed mother who was in her eighties. Her need at that time was to find someone who could help her with a problem related to her late father's Social Security, after she had tried to resolve this problem herself. I helped her find an elder care attorney who, many years ago, was one of the first attorneys in Atlanta who not-only focused on elder care as a specialty, but who had also dealt with Social Security issues on behalf of his clients. He understood the issue and truly wanted to help her. While this problem is not one most people will have, it is just one example of the wide variety of personal and practical issues that widows are faced with after the death of a spouse.

Many times widows are unaware that if she and her husband were both receiving Social Security, a widow can now receive only one Social Security benefit. She is entitled to either her benefit or her spouse's benefit, but not both. Many widows don't know this because it is not something "we are taught in high school," and the issue may not come up in day-to-day discussions until there has been a death. As a result, it may come as quite a shock to a widow that what was the total amount of their monthly Social Security income may now be significantly reduced. The questions surrounding whose Social Security to take—the deceased's or the widow's—and when to begin taking Social Security, is an *extremely* complex issue. It is truly one of the most important financial decisions a widow needs to make after the death of a spouse because once made, the decision cannot be changed.

If neither the widow nor her husband were old enough to apply for Social Security, the right to apply for a Social Security benefit may need to be delayed. If someone is a younger widow, perhaps in her fifties, not being able to apply for Social Security until she is older may be an even greater financial issue for her. Again, it is important for widows to know all the rules concerning when they can apply for Social Security because this can vary. Even then, a decision will need to be made as to whether a widow can afford to delay applying, even if delaying could result in an increased benefit.

Another financial issue for widows to be aware of is that there may be heavy penalties when withdrawing retirement funds, but not necessarily Social Security, before age fifty-nine and a half. As a result couples should consider purchasing life insurance when they are young, and perhaps even term life insurance, which can help them over a financial hurdle, should this situation arise. Most widows who had the opportunity to purchase either term or whole life insurance when they were a couple have found it not only made their life after the death of a spouse much easier, but it made a huge difference. Note: purchasing term or whole life insurance becomes more expensive the older one gets, so the sooner you buy it the better.

Now a little about me and one of the best financially-related discussions my husband and I had. I married for the first time in my early fifties to a man who was also in his early fifties. We had two homes and we sold them both. By combining the proceeds from the sale of our homes, it allowed us to buy a home together for cash that would meet both our needs—such as two spaces for two home offices. The reason we did this was because, being in our fifties, we didn't know what the future would hold. We hoped we would live long lives together. We also hoped we would both continue to work as long as we chose to, but we were also realistic to know that some of our wishes might not happen—one of us could be laid off, one of us could become ill and not be able to work, one of us could die, etc. As it turned out, my husband died unexpectedly due to complications from a heart attack at the age of 61.

One thing I didn't have to worry about financially after his death was making a mortgage payment. We had the good fortune to live in our home mortgage-free for over ten years and I continue to do so. I highly recommend all couples speak with their financial advisor and accountant to determine if buying a home for cash or paying off an existing mortgage would be right for them.

CHAPTER **FOUR** SUMMARY

1. Establish credit in your own name.

2. Find a financial advisor who is willing to work with your level of wealth.

3. Buy adequate life insurance to keep your lifestyle when you and your spouse are young.

4. Don't wait to apply for Medicaid until your money runs out. Seek a professional's help.

5. Don't ask financial questions to care facilities—their interests are different from yours. Ask financial questions to professionals in it.

6. Plan your life in advance instead of taking care of issues as they occur.

7. If you cannot afford to buy long-term care insurance, take advantage of Medicaid by planning early.

8. Make sure your Power of Attorney is up to date to allow someone to step in and manage financial and health affairs for you when you are unable to do so.

9. Buy adequate health insurance for your situation. Seek a professional's help.

10. Remember, once you become a widow, you can only keep one Social Security income.

What's Your Money Story? Find out: **www.ChooseYourMoneyStory.com**

CHAPTER FIVE

Sale of Business

"Charles doesn't go out of a room—he 'makes an exit.'"

—AGATHA CHRISTIE, *Three Act Tragedy*

SMALL BUSINESSES ARE THE LIFEBLOOD OF OUR ECONOMY. They make up 99.7% of all firms and provide 48% of all jobs in the United States. Nationally, Baby Boomers own almost half of all privately held businesses with employees. Six out of ten U.S. business owners plan to sell their company over the next decade.[1] As Baby Boomer business owners retire, our local business landscape is poised to go through a dramatic shift. The effect on their employees and local economy is massive. However, the vast majority (over 85%) of business owners do not have a succession plan in place,[2] and increasingly, many are finding it hard to find a buyer when they are ready to sell.

In this chapter, we'll learn about how to successfully sell your own business before the tsunami of selling companies era arrives!

---

1. project-equity.org
2. project-equity.org

Collect Up Front

I owned the Paper Parlour on Buford Highway for 25 years and sold it in 2002. The first concern I had when I started the business was finding a good location. It was the 1970s. Women were not treated as they are today. They were not taken seriously as business people. Therefore, when I was searching for a location, not only did I have to find a convenient and busy location, but I also had to find a landlord who would rent to me because I was a woman. It was a time of discrimination against women going into business independently without a man. My business partner and I selected two locations, but the only way the landlords would rent to us was if our husbands signed the lease. We did not want to do that. Finally, as our third choice, we found a location on Buford Highway and the landlord accepted us, let us sign the lease, gave us a fair deal just as he would give a man, and treated us equally. We opened our store in a small space on Buford Highway, which was not a fashionable location, but it was an area that was easy to get to and convenient for the customer base we were looking for.

The Paper Parlour was the first party store in Atlanta except for Hallmark Card stores. There weren't any other stores selling party supplies, dispensables, and invitations like ours. There were originally three partners including myself, a woman who knew about this field, and my partner Margie. We had a lot of challenges starting up. We even discovered that our third partner was not honest. She finally admitted to the fact that she wasn't honest and we arranged for her to leave the business. She was only in the business for one year. We did have to pay for her to leave because we didn't want to go to court. I wanted to just focus on growing the business. My other partner, Margie, is still my very close friend, almost like a sister. In looking for a partner, I highly recommend you find one with skills that complement your own skills. It's a little like a good marriage—both partners work well together. My skills are marketing, buying merchandise, and negotiating.

Margie is very personable and crafty, which was excellent for the invitation business. People loved her. We complemented each other in the business. That's very important.

Our business grew and grew. We went from 1,200 square feet and ended up in a huge 15,000 square foot store. We moved three times because we ran out of space, it was so popular!

Our business hit the peak growth right before we sold it. I believe the reason behind our strong growth was that we were a one-stop shop. If you were having a party, wedding, or bar mitzvah, we could do everything from the invitations to setting up at the party. The main thing I always believed in is customer service. No one was to walk into our store without being greeted. We made it a friendly, happy place to be. Having a knowledgeable and friendly staff made each customer feel important. Each customer is important because one customer can tell ten people that they had an excellent experience, or one customer can tell ten people they had a bad experience.

One of the challenges of owning our own business was the employees. Each employee has different needs. Some are motivated by money, some are motivated by personal attention. Some work more than you expect and some don't work to the level you expect. If I had to say the one most challenging thing about running a business, it's the staff.

I woke up almost every day at five in the morning to take care of my three children and husband and prepare my home, then I'd prepare for business. I worked very hard. When my store had grown to almost twenty employees, I realized that I was getting older. I was in my fifties and I thought, "How much more stress can my body take?" I loved the business, but on the other hand, I was working extremely hard and it was very stressful. My partner was at a time of her life when she wanted to do other things as well. We had done very well for ourselves so we decided to look for a buyer. That was a challenge because we didn't want to share with our employees that we were hoping to make a change. On the other hand, we wanted buyers to know that our company was for sale. Privately, we went to a broker.

I looked up retail brokers in the Atlanta area. We interviewed them and listened to their thoughts about our business. It was like looking for a real estate agent for a house. I interviewed a few brokers. We were both very concerned that our employees would find out. We couldn't afford for them to quit or make other plans or treat our customers differently. That was the biggest challenge. It took a few months, but we did find a buyer.

The buyer was a man, which was fine, but he was not open to learning. He hadn't been in that type of business before. He had been in other retail businesses, but he wasn't open to learning about the party business from my partner and me, or from our employees. He didn't treat the employees as we did, either. Against our advice, he moved the store to another location, a fancier location, and he went bankrupt.

We had collected most of the money for the business up front. There was some money for inventory that we did not collect, but I didn't count on that money. I would advise people to get all the money up front. You can never count on money once the company has changed hands.

Sometimes I think that the store was so successful that it could have been a chain like Party City. But I had to make a decision whether to expand nationally or to sell. I decided to sell. Party City came to our market two or three years after we opened. I had to make a decision whether I wanted to spend my whole life working and not being the kind of mother and wife I wanted to be. I still don't know if I made the right decision, but at least I have children and grandchildren who love me. I feel that I took care of my family even though it's hard to balance a career and family.

In regard to risk mitigation, my partner and I had an agreement: it was a buy-sell agreement that would take care of the business and family if one of us passed away. That's very important. We planned for the worse possibilities.

The atmosphere these days is very challenging. I often ask myself whether I would have been as successful if I were running the business now. These days, in addition to local competition, you have national and international competition, not to mention the internet. Had I not sold the business, how would I have been doing financially? I knew that the internet was coming then, but I had no idea how strong it would become. I think that it would be extremely challenging now to run the business. I probably would have had to invest a lot more money again and set up a whole internet strategy. I'm happy I sold it when I did. It was the right time and I've never looked back.

AUTHOR'S NOTES

It's remarkable that Roberta started her own business with partners over forty years ago when there weren't a lot of women in the market. She built a one-stop shop, which was a rare concept then and treated customers well.

When she sold the company, she collected most of the money up front, which is an excellent plan, especially in retail business.

JAN'S STORY:
Do Your Homework Before You Sell

My husband bought our business in 1979 from a woman whose husband passed away. She had very few assets. She had two trucks, three employees, and just a small amount of equipment, but she had a very valuable contract with a company called Milliken and Company. It's a carpet company, and they would only work with preferred vendors. She had the preferred vendor status with the firm and it opened the door for us for more business. That's why my husband was interested in the business. We were married in 1981, and I joined him in the firm. We would put everything we made back into the business. We would go to work at seven in the morning and come home at nine at night. We worked hard, whatever it took to build our business.

We had our first big break in 1985 when Kimberly-Clark came to town. They had a big project and they were looking for someone who could design, install, and maintain their project. They invited three bidders. We worked on it like a college project and bonded with them. Our insurance agent went to Atlanta for us and said to them, "I believe in these people, I believe they can do this project." It was the biggest project we've ever done. It was a $300,000 project in 1985. It was huge. We got the project, we did the work again and again, and it just seemed like that was the biggest step toward growing. After that, we were invited to bid on bigger jobs. That's how we really came to what was the definition of our core business. We would do big jobs while a lot of people do small ones. We did very little residential work. We did mostly commercial or industrial work. Hughes Aircraft came to town right after the project with Kimberly-Clark. We did that project and it just kept rolling. And when Kia came to Georgia, we did a lot of work for them. The economy was working out. The orders just kept coming the whole time we were in business. We didn't leave a twenty mile radius of LaGrange. We turned down more businesses than we accepted because we would only do what we could do and do well.

I had a lot of mentors teaching me how to do accounting, how to work with employees and how to be OSHA safe, basically how to run our company as if we were huge. We were very small, but we operated like we were big. We tried to achieve the same benefit level as the big companies. We had health insurance and a retirement plan. We even provided uniforms. None of the other local landscape companies provided benefits. We retained our employees because of the benefits. Other companies kept rolling them over to us because they had no employee benefits.

We did quite well, but there were a lot of challenges in our business. My husband was 65 and he spent all his time at the office. He's always been a workaholic.

But I noticed a couple of years ago that I was having a harder time getting him in the office to do certain bills. At the same time, running our own business was getting much harder with all the regulations such as DOT, OSHA, and with our employees. In our industry, we can't work when it's raining. That's a lot of stress because if the employees can't work, they don't get paid. As employers we had to sometimes create work for them or loan them money or something, or they would go somewhere else. It's hard to be in a weather dependent business. Additionally, with the advent of email, so many customers turned over purchasing decisions to their head offices instead of a one-on-one contact and having a relationship with us. They didn't know who we were. They didn't know what our qualifications were. They were just going by the numbers and whoever was cheapest would get contracts. That just wasn't how we operated.

With the change of the culture and the increased stress of the business, it was the time for us to look into selling our company. We were young enough to do other things without having all of the drama and the stress. I told him, "The economy is good, our business is good, and I love to travel." We had never been able to take more than ten days off at a time.

We had grown to twenty employees when we sold our business in May of 2019. How did we start the process of selling our business? We approached a business broker who specialized in the landscape industry. Our business was too small to get the big guys to want to gobble us up, but it was way too large to sell to a small person. We were in the middle. One gentleman was not really interested in working with us. He had a large contract come in right after he told us he would work with us, and then he never called us back. We started working with another person and they were calling all the large landscape companies and sending them our stuff. They wanted people who were primarily involved in grounds maintenance. Landscaping is very profitable, but the revenue depends on new projects. Grounds maintenance is the mowing and weeding and the revenue depends on the monthly contract. It's not as profitable as landscape, however it's stable and the company receives monthly payments. It pays the bills. But the creative part is the cream. And when you're trying to sell to a service industry, they don't want this new project based business, they want the stability. They only looked at, "What are your contracts, what is your guaranteed revenue?" And that's what they were interested in. I kept telling them that's not how our industry works. You get your guaranteed income, but this is your cream. Nobody would understand that. They kept approaching these people who are really large companies, but their expertise was the maintenance. They didn't want the landscape.

At the end, we were referred to a business broker who really understood our business. He was looking at our information and he said, "I can sell it." He listed our business on BizBuySell, but didn't put a price tag on it. He just listed the assets since our company was extremely profitable, which is rare for a landscape business. And we had all the benefits and we had the track record, and our profits go up every year. Very few people can say that. We started in December 2018, talking and exchanging information, and he put it on the market in February and sold it in May. That was remarkable, it was really fast and sold at a price that was more than our initial evaluation number.

On our end, I did a lot of research on how to sell a business. My mentor said, "You have to have your records in order, all of your finances need to be in order and timely, and you have to have an active Facebook page. You have to have a presence with a website, and you have to have won awards." Three and a half years ago we made the conscious decision to exit. In order to market the business, I went ahead and established a website, opened up a Facebook page, and applied for the chamber of commerce's business of the year award. For the award, we had to have a mission statement. I thought it was a local award and didn't realize that that was a statewide award. In 2015 we won the award. It was a Troup County Chamber of Commerce, Small Business of the Year. I checked off all items on the list of what I had to do to sell the business and get everything in order. I did my homework and it paid off.

AUTHOR'S NOTES

Jan and her husband had a clearly defined niche market and focus, and therefore, they grew the firm tremendously. They also ran their small company as if they were a large national firm by providing health insurance and a retirement plan, which was rare in her industry.

While many business owners don't listen to advisors, Jan fortified herself with mentors and advisors, listened to them, and did all of the homework before she sold in order to increase the value of their firm. It's a remarkable story.

WISDOM FROM THE EXPERTS AND PROFESSIONALS

Neeli Shah, *Estate and Business Succession Planning Attorney at The Law Offices of Neeli Shah, LLC*

In the next 15 years, the last set of baby boomers are going to hit 75 years of age and transition their businesses. About 60% are closely held businesses. The last statistics I read said about $10 trillion worth of value in businesses will be turned over to the next generation or to third party sales. However, there is a severe lack of planning in this area. I think there is probably going to be a lot of value lost.

One of the most pressing concerns for people as they age are disability and death, and nobody is immune from dying. We frequently see folks who become incapacitated or who pass away without adequate planning. Business owners have to consider that their future plans affect two levels in life. On a personal level, the business tends to be the primary source of income to the family, affecting you and your loved ones. On a business level, it affects your employees and the customers that you serve. When the owner or a partner in a business becomes incapacitated or dies without adequate planning, both levels suffer. In addition, if you've got a partner or a co-owner in your business, they're going to end up taking a hit on the valuation of the business. So the impact of poor planning is not only limited to the owner's family, it can potentially affect the families of other partners, the employees, and the entire community. The impact is exponential.

People don't know what they don't know. We think that we're invincible—we never think that anything is going to happen to us, or we always think we have more time than we do. I have seen cases when an individual is sick and they put things off because planning requires sitting down and asking the serious questions: What is my business worth? What's the correct valuation? Some people would choose, for example, to sell for $5 million outright, instead of getting an appraisal and figuring out what the business is actually worth. It's important to ask yourself, "If I can't get a third party to buy it, how will I transition the business if something happens to me?"

It's also important for partners to have hard conversations with each other. They need to talk about things like: what if one partner needs to buy the other out? What are they going to pay your family? I often hear people say something like, "We've been partners for 15 years. I know that he would take care of my family." Or, "We see each other at church every Sunday and my family will be fine. My partner will take care of them." Instead of planning for the future, people make assumptions and when the worst happens, the people left behind end up struggling. Inevitably, in three to five years, resentment starts building up. The partner is running the business without strategic planning or the vision of the partner who passed away. The surviving partner often ends up sharing the profits with the deceased's family. Resentment builds when you don't have clarity up front, and eventually, bad blood builds up over time.

Most people's goal is for their family to be taken care of, their kids to get along, and for everybody to be happy. If that is truly the goal, then planning and having the hard conversations now is the best way to achieve your dream. When you don't do that, when you leave things to chance, you inevitably end up with miscommunication and resentment. If I expect something from you, but I don't tell you what that is, you're not going to know my expectations.

I have two clients, right now. It's actually a very sad story. It's a couple in their early 40s. The husband passed away. They've got two children ages seven and five. No planning was done. The guy was a real estate developer. He owned several properties and various LLCs. Each was owned with a different partner and different ownership interests. He had no planning and he made no will. Now that he has passed away, under Georgia law, all of his assets and his estates go to probate to be split among his heirs: his wife and children. A lot of business owners don't consider that their personal guarantees have to be dealt with in an estate. Anytime you have an estate, all the debts must be paid off before assets can be distributed to the heirs. This individual had guaranteed a lot of his business debts. Unfortunately, some of these debts were to loan sharks and he was very heavily leveraged. If you don't read and negotiate the terms of your loans over time and maintain them, debt can accelerate. The banks can call the loan essentially. If you have a debt that's been called, the estate becomes the personal guarantor of these debts. Therefore, the estate can't distribute any assets. His wife and children get nothing until all the debts are taken care of. We have to basically liquidate and sell all of his properties prematurely in order to pay the banks. Planning would have affected not only his family, but all of his partners.

We see many situations like this, especially among the immigrant population. The business owner may not maintain the books. Loans are not always documented. There's off-the-record money that has been borrowed from an uncle, siblings, or somebody with the promise of investing, but no paper trail. If you pass away and it's in your name, then that's considered your asset. Without proper planning, this becomes a mess in court for the deceased business owner's family. Much of this could have been avoided by creating a will or a trust that would plan for such a transition.

I have a client whose husband passed away. The two of them owned a company together: the husband owned 75% of the company and the wife owned 25%. Their children were not minors, so it was much simpler case. There were some licensing requirements that the company had to have on an annual basis. The husband always did the licensing under his name alone, instead of listing 75% as his and 25% as his wife's. This caused great aggravation after his death.

M. Everett "Rett" Peaden, *Partner at Smith Gambrell and Russell*

The issue that weighs most on my clients who are women business owners, whether it's articulated or not, is the question of legacy. Whether it's to their family, the community, or the employees at their company, what are they going to leave behind when they pass away? This is especially concerning for Baby Boomer women. Many of them grew up in a world where women weren't routinely business owners, and some of them have been very successful in industries that are traditionally dominated by men: medical practices, engineering firms, general construction, and general contractors. There are very successful women in all of these fields. I think they are particularly keen on preserving their legacy and making sure that they leave a lasting mark and a positive influence for other women who are coming along. Leaving a legacy is really the key concern for them. That trumps money, what their tax return is going to look like, and it motivates a lot of their decisions. These clients often look at a deal or a transaction more holistically than just the bottom line numbers.

I often see a difference between men and women when they are selling their company. When an owner of a business is looking to get out of the business they must look at several different exit plans. They have to weigh whether it makes better sense to sell the business to someone who works in the business, gift it to the next generation—perhaps a child who's interested in the business, or take it to market and try to sell the business to an outsider. When you start talking about outside buyers for a business, there's a big demarcation between strategic buyers. You might be dealing with a competitor, somebody you've done business with in the past, or possibly financial buyers—investors. The typical example of financial buyers is private equity. Private equity is increasingly involved in middle market and lower middle market. A lot of companies, even smaller businesses, are being rolled up by private equity firms. Women-owned businesses may sell to financial buyers, but a definite trend that I've observed is that they gravitate more towards strategic buyers than financial buyers. I think it goes back to the legacy question.

Financial buyers are looking at a short-term turn-around; it's usually no more than five years before they're looking to sell the portfolio of the company. Their goal is maximizing profits. They will come in and get rid of what the financial buyers view as redundancies in the company, even laying off employees. Women business owners, when they're looking at selling the company, generally look at a lot more than just the bottom-line dollars and cents. The company's legacy, the workforce and the families who are supported by it, the type of business that the company does, the markets they serve, and its customers are important for many of my women clients. Strategic buyers understand the market, serve the same customers, and can understand how to keep the business intact better than a financial buyer.

One of the big aspects of selling a company is the due diligence process. Business owners often neglect the due diligence aspect of the company. It's a bit like selling a house. If you fix the roof, put a fresh coat of paint on a house, brand new carpet, and trim the grass, you're going to sell your house for more than you would if it looks like a dump. The same is true for a business. If a business has good records and it's well organized, it's going to sell for more than a business is in disarray. Generally, the businesses owned by women have an advantage. They are often much better organized than businesses owned by men, and that can help the due diligence process. A lot of small companies in particular neglect the due diligence process because they know the company. They don't always keep good records, because they assume they can tell the buyer whatever they need to know. But a buyer isn't going to accept the business owner's story without proof. Keeping good records helps the seller because, during the process, they can give all the information to the buyer in writing and disclose any issues with the business. As the seller, you protect yourself from being sued for things going wrong after a transaction because you've disclosed the problem upfront.

In one situation, I dealt with a business that was owned by two women. They were partners, and they had been in business for a long time. While operating the business, one of the partners had better financing and sources of money than the other partner. Over time, they set up different companies with different ownerships. One part of the business was owned 50/50. Another part was owned 75/25, and another part of the company was owned by only one partner. The group of companies together was one similar business that was going to sell as a whole. When the partners came in to meet with me, it was almost too late. They were already having preliminary discussions with a buyer. They were talking about making the company more presentable and making more sense by shifting some of the assets to different parts of the company. They were trying to decide how to divide up the proceeds of the company. I was able to do a couple things with this client. One was dissuading them from transferring assets without considering the tax implications. I worked with them and their accountant to implement a tax-free reorganization, in which we were able to shift some of the companies around in a different structure and put assets where they needed to be without incurring any taxes up front. And at the end of the day, we had a well-structured company without incurring tax issues, ready for a buyer. They had a selection in place without breaking the S selection, which they were preserving until we got to closing.

When they came to me, they had a letter of intent that they were about to sign. When someone comes in with a letter of intent already signed it's almost too late. Even when the letter of intent is non-binding, you've already set expectations in the letter, and it's really hard to negotiate different points when you've already, in principle, made an agreement. A seller of a business is going to have maximum leverage early in the deal. The further you get along in the deal, the more committed you become, the harder it is to make changes. In this case, I asked them not to sign the letter of intent and we went back to the drawing board. We were able to get a lot of provisions in the letter that protected them later on. When we got to the point of having a purchase agreement, we already knew what was going to be in it and what it needed to look like.

When you're ready to retire, it is critical to get your company ready to sell. Do your due diligence. Involve a lawyer early so that they can help you be the most effective you can be in the sale of your business.

Mark Oldenburg, *Corporate Law Attorney and Partner at Oldenburg & Stiner, P.C.*

Business owners, both sellers and buyers, generally come to see us at two different times and we represent both of them. Sellers, in particular, will come see me very early when they are contemplating a sale. They have not necessarily decided to whom they're going to sell or for how much, but they have been involved in the business for a long time, or they believe it's time to exit. Now is the time to try to sell their business. Sometimes they come to see me when there is a deal on the horizon that they have found a buyer. Often they've already negotiated the purchase price and they need somebody just to help them go through the documents before they close.

At the initial stage, their concerns are primarily twofold. The first and primary concern is "what's the business worth?" A lot of small businesses do not know how much their business is worth on the open market. All businesses are worth what a buyer will pay, but because of the times in which we live and the access to information over the internet, businesses can get an idea what the values are. Some clients come to me and say that they've been told that their business has only book value or it's only worth how much money they have in the bank. They need to really get an understanding of what the business is worth.

The other concern that they have is how to go about selling a business. What steps are involved? We try to coach and counsel business owners through the process of getting an evaluation. The first thing to do is getting your business cleaned up so that you're in a good position to sell it. The analogy we use is that you may have a diamond, but that diamond needs to be polished before you're ready to sell it. Once you are ready to put it on the market, it's time to contact the business brokers. Once there's a deal, you'll need help with preparing the documents for closing.

The probability that small business owners can sell at a price they want usually is zero. By and large, the owners of small businesses, unless they have been keeping up with their values by having a professional who gives them a valuation, generally think that their business is worth more than it is on the open market. Many of them think that it's worth a lot less, and they don't give themselves enough credit. Very, very rarely does a business owner really have a good idea of what the price is going to be at the end of the day.

A few years ago, we had a case in which the business owners wanted to sell both the real estate and the business itself. The buyer and seller had negotiated a purchase price, but when the buyer's attorneys did the title search, they found a problem with the property. Part of the seller's building was encroaching on the neighbor's property. The sellers didn't know that their building was encroaching on the neighbor's land; the neighbors had never complained. The buyer considered calling the deal off. In that circumstance, we were able to set things straight. We found the owner of the neighboring property and we were able to work out a deal with them. After making things right with the property lines the buyer was happy and the deal was still able to close.

Nancy Gault, CPA, *Partner at Nichols, Cauley & Associates, LLC*

In my opinion, the main concern for the business community is finding skilled labor and qualified help to grow the business. Getting employees with a proper education is other issue. I think today a lot of people have a generic education, like liberal arts, history, or something that doesn't necessarily lend itself directly to the job market. Many businesses need more technical skills. Technical training, or training in specific skills is vital today in a world is more technology driven. Education is very important.

Another thing that impacts our communities is family support and life balance. Technology makes this a very instant world. Many people are trying to juggle raising families, having a personal life, a social life, and disconnecting if we can. Balance is hard to find today because of technology. Even if you are away from work, somebody may still call, text you, or email you. As a business owner, there are several other challenges. Health care for a small business is very challenging to provide. With the new law that just passed starting effective 2019, small businesses now can reimburse employees if they're on their spouse's plan for their employee costs. That way they can offer a little bit more affordable care or they can go to healthcare.gov because they are such a small company.

Retaining good, quality employees is a big concern for business owners as well. It's not uncommon for people to call someone else's employees and try to convince them to leave by offering them a raise in salary. How to keep their employees often keeps many business owners up at night.

It's important to talk with a financial planner early. Making financial decisions without talking with a professional can trigger taxes. I had a client who wanted to give her daughter money for a down payment on a house. Luckily, she came to me first. She wanted to sell some stocks. I told her not to sell her stocks because she would have to pay taxes on her gain. At her bracket, capital gains rates could be up to 15% tax. I advised her to gift her stocks to her daughter. The gift was tax free for her. She would have to file a gift tax return, but it would not incur any tax. Her daughter was in a much lower income bracket. By selling the stock the daughter would only pay 5% tax. If my client had sold the stock herself, she would have paid a lot more in investment tax and capital gains tax.

The second story that comes to mind is of a client who did not come to me ahead of time. She was retired and she needed some cash. So, she sold some of her portfolio with high gains, which then triggered taxes. When your adjusted gross income goes to a certain level, you start paying more for Medicare part B. Selling some of her portfolio triggered that. Her husband was ill. They were originally getting a discount on his drugs, which were extremely expensive. Prescription drugs are tied to your adjusted gross income. When she sold the stocks, she triggered investment tax, she now has to pay more in Medicare part B, and their prescription drug costs are five times higher than before. She is considering not giving him that drug anymore because of the expense. My advice to them was to borrow money against their portfolio and not cash it out—borrow and take a line of credit against it. They could easily get a line of credit with their stocks and bonds.

Then, over time, they can sell stocks that stay below the limits and pay back that loan.

In regards to selling a business, it's important to understand the structure of the deal before negotiating it. Some structure is capital gains and some is ordinary tax. A lot of business owners think that the whole business will sell at capital gains, and that's not true. You have to recapture depreciation at ordinary rates. There are different ways of structuring a deal. I try to let the owners know that they should not be concerned with the sales price. The important thing is how much cash they get after tax. Sometimes you can take a smaller sales price, and if the deal is structured correctly, you'll end up with more cash.

A lot of people accept the price of the business before really understanding its true worth. Sometimes, women will undervalue their business worth. Don't set the sales process too quickly. Make sure you really understand the parameters of the business. Understand what the market is, who your competitors are, if they are growing or not, and whether they could get a strategic value, which is different than a fair market value. A fair market value is when one person comes in, buys the business and does the same thing with the business. Essentially, they've just replaced one owner for another. That's a fair market value. A strategic value is when a buyer wants to do a roll up. They buy many of the same types of businesses for more market share, or they're looking to expand their line and your business would complement what they're doing. That brings more money to the table, but a lot of owners do not understand who the buyer is. The buyer who has a true strategic purpose pays a little bit more.

Right now the buzz is that if you have a home, you should

think about selling. Sell now while the market is high. If you have a business that is related to the real estate industry, now might be the time to sell because the business is going to be softening. It's important to know where you are in the cycle, the economy, and what businesses you're related to so that you don't sell too soon or too late. Know the right time to sell.

When you're thinking about selling, work closely with a business broker or find someone to sell for you. A lot of people will list their business with a broker and just hand it off. This is a bad idea. You've got to understand what the broker is doing and how they're presenting your information. It's worth your time to be active in the process. Another option is to hire a consultant such as a financial planner or a CPA valuation expert to work with that broker. This assures that the information is presented correctly and fairly. When the offers come, the broker wants to sell your business as quickly as possible to get it off of their inventory and make their commissions; they're not emotionally attached to that business. Sometimes you need to have someone to independently look at the deal and ask questions like, "Was that a fair offer?"

It's very common for investors to make low-ball offers. Several business owners just run for a couple of years, flip the business, and sell for higher. You need someone to advocate for you with the broker. Then, you're not directly tied to the process. It's kind like selling your own home. You're emotionally tied to the property. You have to have someone else selling it for you. Not always, but women are more often peacemakers and not good negotiators. They don't like the negotiation. If somebody is being aggressive, then they often just want to be done with the process and won't negotiate. They need to step away and let someone else be that negotiator for them.

There's a fine line between selling too low and missing the opportunity. Having a third party who can assess the many angles of the deal can help you make a good sale.

Long-term planning and bringing someone in to help get that business ready for sale is important. This may take years. I'm talking about getting the books clean, "Let's get it vanilla." Keep your business separate from your personal life. If you need personal money, write yourself a check, don't run your personal expenses through the business. Get clean books. Make sure that your expenses are categorized the same way year after year. It brings you more value. The buyer has more confidence in your numbers if they are well organized, and that brings you a higher value. Changing the way you organize your expenses each year creates chaos and you won't bring as much money with that.

If you sell a business, chances are that you're not going to get all cash up front. You will likely get some cash now and the rest will be paid over time. Make sure that the buyer is personally liable. Sometimes the buyer will use the business as collateral: if the buyer doesn't pay, you can get the business back. This is not a good plan. You won't get the same business back as when you were running it. Make the buyer personally liable on that note. If the business does badly and they cannot run the business, they will still have to pay you for it.

Once you have sold the business, give yourself a moment. Park the money somewhere for maybe six months or more. It does not need to be placed in a long-term investment that you can't get your money out of. In other words, keep it liquid. I am not saying that you can't put it in the stock market. It needs to be liquid, and it needs to sit there for a while so that you can emotionally unwind and think clearly about the next steps. Take the emotion out of the money. Take time to understand what your spending habits are and how much money you really need to live. Consider these questions: Am I going to totally retire? Am I going to semi-retire? Am I going to go back to work full-time? Those are three difference environments. Understanding your cash requirements will help you make the decision of what to do with your money.

Additionally, if this is the only money you have, if you have to retire, you'll want to be able to live off of your investment's earnings. If you keep spending the principal, after a while you're going to run out of money. If you're eighty years old, that might not be a concern. But if you are sixty-five or seventy, you could still have twenty years to live. Work with a good financial planner who can help you determine your cash requirements for the year. Some people look at the numbers and decide they can sell their house, downsize, and need a little bit less and be set for retirement. Some decide they don't want to sell their house. They know they'll need to go to work part-time. These are the decisions that most people can't make until six months to a year after selling their business.

Another issue people face when they come into money is loans to family and friends. Women tend to be very soft-hearted towards their children and friends. Sometimes, after the sale of a business, people come around asking to borrow money. Next thing you know, you've given too much money away. My recommendation is not to loan money to friends and family. Tell them that your money is tied up. If you really feel that your adult child has a valid need, suggest that you'll help them get a bank loan. Put up collateral for that loan, but don't let them know about it. In this case the bank is loaning the money to the child, and as a result the child will feel more obligated to pay back the loan. They don't know that mom put the collateral up, but now they have a bank note that they've got to make. This takes the pressure off the mother-child relationship.

Jayden Doye, CPA, *President of Prestige Accounting Solutions*

The number one pressing issue my clients face when selling a business is determining the selling price. People don't know how much their business is worth and they don't know what the multiple should be. The pricing of your business depends on a valuation, and that valuation is going to determine what the multiple should be. In certain industries there is a standard multiple that determines the price of the business. Accounting businesses for instance: accounting firms, on average, are sold at a multiple of 1.25 their annual revenue. If an accounting firm brings in a revenue of $100,000 on an annual basis, the average selling price would be $125,000. That's the industry. Many people don't know that. It's important to work with a business broker or a lawyer with a good reputation who can help with these issues.

Another difficult issue is walking away from the business. Often, people sell their business because they are retiring. If you have spent the last forty years of your life building a business up from the ground, it can be very difficult to walk away. Removing the emotional tie to the business is hard for many people.

The business does become a person's identity. I recommend that my clients begin to separate their face from the business. The business should be able to stand without them. People should not have to come to my clients with problems. That's a sign of a successful business. It also helps them know when to sell the business. There are so many different factors that come into the timing of selling a business that people don't know about, like the time of year, or the economy for example.

The number one financial issue my clients are concerned about is taxes. This is what keeps most business sellers up at night—it's the same for millions of Americans. Selling a business, most commonly through asset sale, brings about tax implications. A lot of people don't do tax planning properly. When you're selling a business there is going to be a large tax liability. The way you go about the sale of the business determines whether it will be seen as ordinary income or capital gains. There are so many different factors involved. People who don't do proper tax planning will not be aware of the potential liabilities until it's time to file their tax return. Without proper planning, they are often unaware of what their tax rate is and how much should be given to the IRS and the state. Just the thought of having to pay a large amount makes people very uncomfortable.

Another concern is how to maintain their lifestyle after selling the business. If someone is used to a certain lifestyle because of their business income, and not having that income can be devastating. Navigating what retirement actually looks like is very difficult for people. When there are partners involved, splitting the proceeds among the partners can trigger some discord among the team. Many businesses don't have good accounting records and do not keep up with the reconciliation of the equity accounts of the partners' capital accounts. When it comes to dissolving the business, giving people their equity and the proceeds of the business, poorly kept records or if one partner has negative equity in the business, can cause huge issues.

I helped one of my clients out of an entanglement in which she sold a restaurant but didn't tell me until the next calendar year. The sale was considered an asset sale and it fell under section 1060 of the IRS code. And when you have a sale that falls under that law, you have to file form 8594. This form has different lines for the different classes of assets that are sold: fixed assets, inventory, furniture and equipment, intangibles, good will etc. This ideally should be filed during or right after the sale because that's when all of the information is fresh. Unfortunately, she didn't tell me personally until the year after and in filing her tax return, that form had to be filled out and I had to work backwards.

In this case, I had to retroactively finish financial statements for the business. This is very difficult and time consuming, and I had to work backwards to file form 8594. In order to complete that form, I had to do extensive research, reading through the thirty-page contract of sale, and doing a proper assessment of the ending inventory and ending fixed assets. Then it was necessary to compare what the contract said versus what I could see in the accounting system. There were also liabilities that hadn't been paid but were part of the sale of the business. Everything had to be compiled into various accounting journal entries so that I could complete the form. In the end, I was able to help the taxpayer as well as the purchaser who also had to include that on his tax return.

What I have learned over the years is that it's best to work with professionals who have experience in your specific industry when it comes to buying and selling. If a business broker has never sold a restaurant and has, for example, only worked in the real estate industry, that's not the person you want to work with. The person who handled this case originally was simply a friend of my client and they really dropped the ball. It's also important to do your own research. Thoroughly read documents, especially the lines that include numbers. In this case, certain things weren't included in the contract that actually happened in the sale of the business.

In this case, the broker and the lawyer were the same person; a friend of hers who didn't charge her. Never accept free work.

Many mistakes are made in poor preparation. As business owners, we feel like "I've built this business from the ground, I know what I'm doing." However, often it's worth bringing in a consultant, someone who specializes in helping businesses get ready for sale. By not properly preparing your business for sale two years in advance, you are essentially going to undermine the sale and you are devaluing the business.

Timing is important. Selling the business at the wrong time can become a big problem. Sometimes, elections can play a part in the sale of a business because different political parties and different presidents have different views on tax rates and things of that nature. Additionally, selling a business when the economy is down makes a difference. I do not recommend selling a business during a pandemic unless you have to, but some people have done so. When you sell a business during a pandemic or when the economy is down, you're essentially limiting the number of buyers. Many people don't want to buy a business when the economy is down because it's high risk. You're missing out on a lot of money because it is unlikely you'll be able to sell the business for as much as you could if you sold when the economy was up.

Often it's not a health issue that causes someone to sell at a bad time, it's just that someone doesn't want the business anymore. However, two years ago they knew they didn't want to run the business anymore. They should have started planning back then.

Sara Burden, *President of Walden Businesses Inc.*
At the present time, the most pressing issue in the business

community is Baby Boomers who have held on to their businesses for too long. Then the pandemic happened. A lot of these owners may decide to try to ride it out one more year, their businesses will likely begin to lose some of their revenue, their profitability, and they will be less attractive to the potential buyers in the marketplace. By holding on too long, many business owners will lose some of their value.

We like to be able to go into a company anywhere from three to five years before they're ready to sell so that we can take a look at their financial situation. If it's a manufacturing environment, we want to look at what the equipment is like and what the inventory is like. A lot of times they've been holding on to dead equipment that's no longer used. It may be off the balance sheet, but it's still sitting in that factory. The same thing is true about inventory. If the inventory is not current, it will not have value. No one is going to pay for old inventory. We like to have them start with those simple things to clean up first. At the same time, we'll look at what their financial picture looks like to a potential buyer. They need to work with their CPA to clean up the balance sheet and to make sure that they can produce three to five years of good PNLs and balance sheets that are consistently written.

Unfortunately, a lot of small business owners who have $50 million or less in revenues are guilty of using Quick-Books to keep their financial records. And unless they're a well-trained accountant or they've hired a CFO to take care of their records, an owner can easily mess those records up. You'll see things like a cash-base balance sheet and an accrual-based P&L. That's a deadly mistake when you get into due diligence. Oftentimes we see a seller who keeps their own financial records in QuickBooks. We have to go into that with greater scrutiny than if they have a CPA who is checking their work every month, or they have a CFO onsite who is making sure that things are handled properly.

We want to be able to show a potential buyer good accurate information, not just for one year, but for at least three years, preferably five. Many smaller businesses qualify for an SBA loan when they are ready to sell, which would take them up to $5 or $6 million in value. Their financial statements must align with their tax returns because SBA is only going to look at the tax returns. A lot of privately held businesses run personal items through their PNL, and if the tax returns can't demonstrate that the taxes were paid on those items, then the day of reckoning is the day that loan is made. At that time the business owner either has to make a correction to the tax returns or pay the taxes they have not paid. It is far better to do your financial records correctly all along and paying the taxes as you go.

The pressing issues that keep most business owners up at night are usually employee related. They may worry about losing a key employee, not finding a replacement, or getting them trained. Sometimes it is a financial issue that the business owners are concerned about. Perhaps their markets have changed, but the owner has not changed with the markets. The demands are in one direction now, but they haven't made any changes with the changing demands. That's a financial issue. We often see in a situation where there are heavy cost of goods components on the financial statements that the owners are not watching the margins and slowly they're paying more for their cost of goods and they haven't raised their prices for their customers. As a result, their margins are eroding. That erosion naturally erodes the bottom line. And particularly if they're older, they don't have the energy to put into the business anymore. They trust others to make key decisions and assume that what's being done is in their best interest. And oftentimes it's not. As long as you own a company, you cannot lose sight of what your customers need, what you're giving your customers, what those margins are, and your general and administrative expenses.

I can give you one example of a client. They are in a market that really enjoyed a good economic time. The time has changed. They were in a construction-related business, and when they came to us, their books and financial records were in such bad shape that we could make neither heads nor tails out of them. We couldn't sell the business as it stood. We recommended that they give their records to a good CPA. They needed to be able to give us three years of good financials. They came back to us recently with beautiful financial statements, everything backed into itself and was consistent. We had an offer on the table within a very short time. Considering this business is in an industry going through some changes, this sale was very gratifying. They listened to our advice and it paid off.

Another client that I've worked with and known for a number of years does not have such a stellar story. This was a great business. It was successful, it had a nice profit margin, and a very good reputation. However, it had a problem we did not know about until after we had multiple offers on the business and we couldn't close a deal. We could get them almost to the closing table and the deals would fall apart. Quite by accident learned that a key employee, who had been with the company since the day it started, was sabotaging those deals. This person was a key player in the company and wanted to maintain the control that he had in the company after the owner retired. He enjoyed his own little life and was making quite a bit of money from the company. It was a bad situation.

I finally had to tell the owner that he had to get rid of the employee and replace him with someone he could trust, or he had to find a way to pay the employee off and make him play ball the way he should have been playing ball.

The owner hasn't done anything yet and he's now 74. That's a bad story. It could be a beautiful story, but unfortunately, the owner has not listened. Multiple buyers have told him about the problem, too. If this continues, he may pass away before the business can sell, turning the whole mess over to his wife, and she'll have to deal with it. And I can't imagine any loving husband wanting to do that to his wife.

I want to share another story. We had a client who had a good manager running the business for him. But, he was a day trader and was killed in a shooting. There were multiple people killed that day and he was one of them. And he had not signed power of attorney over to anyone. We had to take the business off the market because it had to go through probate. By the time they finally got through the probate process, the business had deteriorated so badly without his management.

We have had situations in which our clients have come to us saying, "I have terminal cancer. I need you to help me sell this business. I don't want to leave this responsibility to my family." In cases like this we've got to work quickly. We've got to have enough time to get a new owner in there and transition the business and those relationships to the buyer. That was a crisis situation because of a health issue.

Eric Togneri, *Managing Director at Neri Capital Partners*

For most business owners, their businesses are wrapped up in the majority of their life's work. They've typically spent decades building a company before it changes hands. This is new territory where, for the most part, they have never been. Very few business owners are what you'd call "serial entrepreneurs" who regularly start and sell companies. In most cases, business owners have just one company and this is the only time they have been through the selling process. The stakes are high and it's something that they're not necessarily comfortable with because they've never experienced it before.

On average, according to the SBA (small business administration), 85% of the average business owner's net worth is in the value of their company. They're relying on it, not only for their well-being on a day-to-day basis, but also for their retirement. Life and legacy become intertwined with the company. We call it a liquidity event when somebody sells their company, and that 85%, depending on how it's structured, becomes cash.

Ultimately the market will tell us what the business is worth, but we utilize very sophisticated software for business valuations. There are qualitative factors to consider as well, such as recurring revenues, how big the business is, and the money that can be counted on. Customer concentration is another thing to look at. Consider, for example, CVS and Walgreens. Five of these stores could be 60% or 70% of your business. Obviously, that adds more risk because if you lose the Walgreens account, you lose a significant amount. One complication in business valuation is that it's not like selling a home. You have a pretty good idea of what your home is worth based upon similar properties. In selling a business, there is no real benchmark that's publicly available because most companies are privately held. There are many factors that feed into the value of a business. Our job is to look at those factors and give a business owner an idea of what to expect in terms of how much their business is worth. Ninety-eight percent of business owners have never had a business valuation done. Typically, their perception of the value of their company is skewed. The business is a big part of their lives. They have put all of their emotional and physical energy into building this company and it's hard for them to look at it from a third party perspective.

I have two stories to share with you, one good and one bad. I'll start with the good one. We had a client who owned a glass and glazing company, who came to us through a referral from a company in Nashville, Tennessee that we had sold. This company was in Roanoke, Virginia. The business owner was thinking about selling the company. He had a really good work and personal life balance. He had put together such a great management team that he could go on vacation literally for a month or two. He did often travel to Europe and other places. He was never completely out of the business. He would call in every day and he would make major decisions, but he had a great management team that he trusted and empowered. The company didn't require his physical presence. That made his company very valuable to a third party. Ultimately a company in Michigan came in and bought it. He did a lot of things right: one was having a good management team in place, the other was empowering his people. He had an extremely successful company doing the glass and glazing worth for several large businesses and universities. Selling the business was a very successful transaction because the owner was ready to sell the company.

He financed part of the sale himself, which we call owner financing. He spread some of his capital gains out over time and that allowed him to get an even a better price for his company. That part was really good from the perspective of it enabled him to be in charge and remain active in the business.

He managed the business full time for about six months, and then he was just kind of on call to answer questions as needed. His management team was really the key. It was private equity that came in and bought his company: an investor, not a competitor. In order to maintain continuity, they wanted to keep the management team that had been in place for decades. So, they structured a deal in which the management team got a percentage of the company and incentives to stick around. The private equity firm didn't have a tight timeline or mandate such as turning around and selling in five years. They did not have a firm date, but they had it in mind to sell around the five year mark. It was a successful transaction all around.

In this situation, the keys to their success was having a great team in place and empowering them in their work. Then the business becomes a real company. If the owner is the company, then the company becomes less valuable.

Bad sales situations typically come from a lack of planning. In an ideal world, I meet a business owner five to ten years before they actually want to sell their business. In this case, the likelihood is high that they'll get a very good asking price. The reason you need that time is because, unlike real estate property where you can go in and fix a lot of issues in a relatively short amount of time to improve the value of the property, the value of a company takes years to improve. One of our clients was an avionic shop in Nashville Tennessee. Avionics are basically all the computer systems that go into flying planes. It was a very successful company that had been in business for three decades, received every award that you could imagine in the avionics field. It was the top avionic business in the country and people would fly in from all over. Most of their customers weren't from Nashville—they literally had folks flying in from Saudi Arabia to have their planes worked on.

The owner of the business was getting older, in his mid-seventies, when he decided he would consider selling. This decision was driven by a health issue and he had not planned for it. He did not have an empowered team of individuals managing his company. He had a lot of experienced people working for him, but he made all the decisions. Just as he was ready to put the company on the market, he passed away. The company naturally went to his wife, who had worked a little bit in the business, mainly administrative work. She wasn't running the company, she wasn't an avionics person, but she helped manage the office and she was involved. The leadership was gone, and the company had not been prepared for that possibility. In the end, a company that was worth about $10 million, ended up selling for just over a million. They lost about 90% of the value of the company as a result of no planning. There was certainly time for the owner to plan; it wasn't an abrupt death in his forties or fifties. But he just never made the plans. The family was okay, but literally, millions were left on the table that could have gone to his children or their church.

Don H. Bravaldo III, *President at Bravaldo Capital Advisors*

There are myriad problems that business owners face when preparing to sell their business, but I would say that the number one problem that we see time and again is a failure to plan. It takes an average of six months to a year to conduct a professional sales process. Oftentimes it can take three to five years to prepare a business for a successful exit.

The world seems to be divided in the timing of coming to

see me. I see the 80-20 rule that most people have heard of at work. Only about 20% of the people I meet will plan. They may be three years away from retirement, ready to do something else, and it's time to sell the business. It's time to plan for an exit: putting the financials together and making sure that they have a successful management team in place. Only about 20% of clients will take three to five years to plan to exit their businesses professionally and do it with enough time to manage it effectively. The other 80% of the people that I encounter are reactionary. They let events drive the decision to sell the business. Usually the three D's: death, divorce, and discouragement are big drivers of this 80%. For example, let's say an advisor calls me and says, "A business owner who's founded the business and has been running it for thirty years just died. Now the widow owns the asset and doesn't know how to run the business. Can you sell the company?" We can, but I use the analogy of flying an airplane: if you give us a long runway, then we can take off and we can land smoothly. If you give us a short runway, we'll figure out how to get the plane up and we'll land it, but it's going to be bumpy and not the best landing.

It makes a big difference when people plan. Companies are valued on cash flows and whether or not they have been depressing the income for tax reasons. If they just wait until they get an offer, a buyer is going to look at those financial statements and offer a low number. A lot of business owners don't value getting professional help. Oftentimes I think it's because they were taken advantage of by professionals early on. Sometimes an entrepreneur's large ego gets in the way. They run their business successfully so they believe they can also sell their business successfully, do their own accounting, legal, and financial planning. But that's not the case. These are very specialized processes. I would say that the most common mistake owners make is when they are ready to sell. If they haven't met a company like ours, oftentimes in a hot mergers and acquisitions market, they sell to the first buyer who knocked on the door and made an offer. The reality is that value is often in the eye of the holder. A company is really only worth what somebody is willing to pay for it. But had they sought professional help, they could have had a better deal.

There are a million examples of success from the 19 years that I've advised private business owners in the world of mergers and acquisitions. But still, to this day, one of the worst cases that I recall was a business owner who had very unfortunate timing. He had a successful business in the metal roofing fabrication industry and roll forming of steel, which was a metal component for roofing systems. He had taken that business over from his father. Unfortunately, this was prior to the recession. In 2007 they decided to open some recreational vehicle dealerships. They used the metal roofing business to secure bank loans on the RV dealers. When we went into the recession, RV dealers performed terribly. Many dealers went under and that jeopardized my client's core business. The owner personally guaranteed a mountain of debt. The bank started a foreclosure process to force the business owner to raise the capital to pay for the RV dealerships.

We were brought in to help sell the business at the wrong time. It wasn't the right time to sell a good business, but we had to in order to protect the owner's personal wealth. During that process, we ultimately sold the business. The owner was depending on that asset to retire and ultimately we sold it for the amount of the debt involved. We kept the owner from losing personal wealth, but that owner had to start all over at age 62, working for somebody else in order to save for retirement.

While it was a success story in terms of our role in selling the company, it was also sad to see someone having to start over at that age. Bad timing, poor planning, and just bad luck.

Most private businesses are owned by Baby Boomers. Baby boomers are getting near retirement age, but we have expected them to be net sellers for many years. Many of them have started too late on that process to get the maximum value. Can we help a business who hasn't taken three to five years to sell properly? Yes. In some cases these businesses are more prepared than others. Sometimes we meet with a business that has been professionally managed. They have a chief marketing officer, chief sales officer, chief financial officer, in addition to the owner as a president. They have a really good management team. They have outside accountants who do audits of the company. They have a diversified customer base and these companies are prepared to sell. In fact, that's what a private business owner should be doing. In theory, they should be running their business every day as though they're going to sell the business. But that's not typical.

There was a business a few years ago that we worked with. It was a fantastic business—a manufacturing firm. There were multiple owners: one group of owners wanted to sell, and another group of the owners wanted to continue to grow the business. The business was growing so fast it needed additional capital. Ultimately, knowing that one group of owners wanted to leave, reluctantly, they all agreed that they would recapitalize the company, change some of the ownership, and bring in professional capital. One of the managers met a private equity group at his country club. He told them about their problems with selling the company and needing capital to continue to grow. The private equity group made an offer and they spent about four months negotiating with the group directly. About three weeks from closing the transaction, the private equity group changed the deal. They had an issue with the working capital, which is a very common issue. Often this issue comes up after the sale, but in this instance it was before. The deal broke down, and the closing didn't go through.

At that point someone introduced the owners to us. Their first mistake was not preparing to sell the company. They hadn't really thought through how they wanted to sell. The second mistake, probably the most critical was, making the mistake of dealing with only one buyer. We were able to run a professional sales process. We got the books and records straight to prepare for due diligence, we put professional marketing in place, and researched the right buyer. We also ran an auction-style confidential sales process in which about sixty different companies bid. Within a six month timeframe we doubled the valuation that the owners had received from the original private equity group offer and we closed on the sale of the company.

Dan Jordan, *VP of National Sales and Business Development at The Oxford Highland Group*

In the business community, the biggest challenge for many people who want to sell their businesses is discovering their business isn't ready to sell. Often, the main challenge with small businesses is that the business owner is very much needed in the day-to-day operations, especially for sales and growing new business. Many of my clients want to deal with the owner. When that happens, the owner really doesn't have a business, what they have is a job. If they were to go away and leave for any significant amount of time, immediately the business would stop growing. Soon it would start declining.

That's not something you can sell. A buyer will not want to acquire an asset if a company is dependent on the original owner's presence.

I would say that 90% of small businesses are actually people who own their own jobs. Some companies, for instance trucking companies, can make good money—$300,000 to $400,000 a year. But with certain businesses like this, you make money while you own it. However, you won't make money when you sell it. Other businesses, like a software or web design company, will make no money while you're building it. You're borrowing money just trying to keep things going. Then suddenly the company turns a corner and you sell at a huge profit. Some businesses that you grow to sell and some businesses you earn your money while you own it, then you just close it down.

Business owners need to learn how to turn their job into a business. It's not difficult. I've learned this through making my own mistakes. I've had seven businesses. I am really good at growing a business, but I'm a terrible manager. I'm not interested in that stuff. So, I'll grow a business to a certain level and then I sell it. That's what I do. I should have been smart and listened to my wife. She said, "Why don't you just hire a manager to run that place for you. Let them do the operation, then you can go out and sell? That's what you're good at. And that's what you like doing." No, no, no, I told her. I didn't think I could trust anybody. However, that's exactly what people should do. How do you change your business? You do what you're good at, then hire other people to do the rest. It makes so much sense. But people like me often think that we have to be in control of everything.

I have one client right now who has five or six stores that sell a certain product. She and her husband used to run the entire business. Then they got divorced. At one time she was the face of the business and doing all the marketing and advertising. Now she has to come in and handle the operations. Very quickly revenues were cut in half. Now she's asking, "What do I do?" The real question is, "What will happen if you do nothing?" The answer: in six months, she'll be out of business if she does nothing.

To save an enterprise, sometimes you have to make some hard choices. You may have to let go of some of your employees or some expenses. Sometimes there are decisions you have to make quickly, right at the beginning, in order to stop the cash bleed. Perhaps you have a key employee who's making a whole lot of money. In order to save the business, you may have to end their employment. When you do, all of a sudden you've got a whole lot of money in hand. And if you do that right away in an emergency situation, you get more revenue right away.

I often hear the question: how do I get more revenue? There are probably some things that you used to do when you first got started that you're not doing now. Go out and visit clients. Ask for referrals. Go out and network. Ask for the order. Get your employees to start asking for the order. You are essentially starting over. Six months from now you will have something to sell.

A lot of people become very complacent. They've built their business up to a certain level. They don't see themselves as the type of person who has to go out and drum up business anymore or do menial tasks in their own company. They think that's embarrassing. But what is more embarrassing? Poverty in America. That's embarrassing. It's not embarrassing to sweep floors. It's the exact opposite. You don't have to do it forever. But, if you start thinking that's embarrassing, that certain tasks are beneath you, then you're already out of business.

Here's a good question I ask all my sellers because they always want more money for their business. The seller usually has a number in their head for what they think their business is worth. The question I always ask them when they give me a number is this: would you pay that for your business? Be honest with yourself. Would you pay that? That's what you're asking someone else to give for your business. If the answer is no then you're not going to be able to sell it. The next question to ask yourself is: what would your business have to do for you to be willing to pay that amount for your own business? The answer to that question can cause changes and that can result in growth. We set up the systems and processes and get it growing again. That's when it is time to sell.

Dennis Brown, *Partner at PACE Capital Advisors*

Two primary challenges for business owners are people and the economy. It can be very difficult finding good people as a business continues to grow. Technology changes and companies need people who are able to keep up with the changes to the way business is done. The other question that poses challenges is: What is it going to happen with the economy? What is going to happen in an election? It varies from industry to industry what business owners are worried about.

Oftentimes, a business owner doesn't truly understand the value of their business or what they need out of the business in order to maintain a certain lifestyle in retirement. I always ask my clients if there are any personal items they run through the business and so forth. And it's not unusual that they tell me their books are clean, that there's nothing "major" on them. But when we start looking, we find cell phones, cars, insurance, extended vacations, and meals. It may be only $30k to $50k a year, but over a period of twenty years, you're talking about close to a million dollars or more taken in personal expenses. This lowers the value of the company. They don't think about that part of the equation.

I group the market in three segments. One segment I call the 60% Group. That's the vast majority of business owners. Their attitude is, "I'm not going to listen to advice." Unless there's a motivating factor such as health concerns, they don't seek proper advice. The second segment is the 5% Group who seek out good advice from a professional on day one. They immediately began to align themselves with good trusted advisors and begin developing their management team. The management team begins and over time is able to do more of the day to day operations of the business. As a result, the owner can remove themselves from the day-to-day operations. At that point in time, that business becomes more readily transferable because the value of the business is not dependent upon the owner. The third group is what I call the 35% Group. They are coachable; they know they need help but they oftentimes just don't know where to start. They ask "What's the process?" It all just seems overwhelming.

The 5% Group is the best operators. They typically have a good core of trusted advisors; they have removed themselves from the daily operations of the business, so it becomes more transferable. Oftentimes they are ready to sell at any point in time. The big issues for the 35% group or the 60% group is planning for the future. What happens to the business if something happens to them? Most business owners don't have a plan.

When I ask whether or not they have a continuity plan, often their response is yes. They have life insurance. That plays an ethical role, but it doesn't answer the question. Would the business survive? Think about all the negative things that could happen. Your competition is immediately going to start poaching your good people and spreading rumors to your customers. Your key management team is going to wonder whom they should report to: a son or daughter? A spouse? They have a family to take care of. They are a commodity in the marketplace and if they have a good track record, the competitors are going to approach them. If there is any uncertainty, the decision becomes relatively easy for good employees to leave. They will also be worried about whether or not the business will be sold. What's will happen to their jobs? By not having a plan, you will not only lose customers, you'll also lose employees. If you're borrowing money from a bank and a personal guarantee, you may also lose your line at the bank. Nothing scares the bank more than surprises. The bank may freeze your working capital line. You also have to consider your vendors. They may change their terms if your company seems to be in trouble. Now, not only are you losing employees and customers, you've lost your bank line and the support from your vendors. All of this could be avoided if you'd simply made a contingency plan from the beginning.

The value in the business can deteriorate rapidly. According to the University of Connecticut Family Business Center, 47.7% of the transition and ultimate demise of the firm was precipitated by the founder's death. What that really means is the owner didn't have a plan. We work with a business owner in helping them address two critical areas for a contingency plan: Ownership (What do you want to happen to the business?) and Leadership (Who's going to run the business?) The answer to that question may not necessarily be the majority stockholder. You need somebody to run the business and take the anxiety out of the workforce. Your key management team will handle operations, but how do you incentivize them to stay around? Who's going to write the checks? Who will step into your shoes in a worse-case scenario and how will they access important details like passwords, combinations, keys, etc. By virtue of having a plan, you're locking down your management team and the banks will not be as concerned. They're going to watch the business like a hawk, but by having a plan, you've taken a big risk off the table. They're going to support you. The same is true of your vendors. Your business has a reasonable chance of surviving and reaping the value that you created out of the business by virtue of having a plan and addressing those areas.

About five or ten years ago, I was talking to an owner who was thinking about transitioning the business to his son. The question in a case like this is, how do you structure a deal to minimize taxes and get the value you need out of the business to set your financial goals for retirement? When he came to see me, the guy was in good health. There were a lot of different ways to structure the deal. But he couldn't make a decision. He talked about making the decision over a period of six months. We talked through several strategies that would get him the best deal. But he never made the plan for the transition. Unfortunately, he became seriously ill and passed away six weeks later and nothing ever happened. His son inherited the business. At that point in time, the company was worth about $35 million. But because plans hadn't been put in place to transfer the business in a tax-efficient manner, the son had to deal with estate planning issues including hefty estate tax.

CHAPTER **FIVE** SUMMARY

1. Make sure your business partners are honest.

2. Focus on customer service.

3. Do your research on how to sell a business. Don't try to sell your business to someone who knocked on the door first.

4. Meet with an Estate and Business succession planning attorney to get your affairs in order.

5. Do not wait till a death or disability occurs to make plans for your future.

6. Be organized with your financial records and tax returns. Show consistency over a period of three to five years to increase valuation.

7. Get your business cleaned up. Eliminate personal expenses from your business records.

8. Hire the right people. You can't grow your business without finding quality help.

9. Understand where your company is in the business cycle so that you do not sell too soon or too late.

10. Work closely with a business broker to understand how your information is being presented to potential buyers and hire a financial planner or CPA valuation expert. They will ensure your information is presented correctly and fairly.

11. Put together a great management team and empower them to make decisions, so your company can run without you.

12. Hire a business consultant three to five years before you are ready to sell the business.

What's Your Money Story? Find out: **www.ChooseYourMoneyStory.com**

FINAL COMMENT

CONGRATULATIONS ON READING THROUGH THIS BOOK! I hope that you learned something you didn't know that you can apply to your life.

Your next step is to take action. First you need to visualize your ideal future and list the things you need or want to do to make it happen, i.e., action plan. You may want to come up with a best case scenario, normal case scenario, and worst case scenario, and make sure that your future will be OK even with the worst case scenario. You have to talk to yourself first and have a deep and honest conversation. Then take actions on your action plan such as contacting your attorney, mediator, psychologist, Medicare specialist, or wealth manager. Your life will not improve without taking actions even though you gain great knowledge.

Also know your limitation. If you are not comfortable to handle on your own, use professionals. That is why they are there. I would never try to be my own doctor or CPA—why is it that so many of us believe we can save money by trying to do other, very complicated things on our own just because we can READ? It's insane. Good attorneys, like good doctors, will refer clients to more specialized professionals when their knowledge is not for cases so in depth.

As Benjamin Franklin quotes, "Words may show a man's

wit but actions his meaning." Let's start something to change your current situation for a better future.

For our readers, I offer *"Your Money Story"* **Worksheet** as a digital gift. You can get it at: **www.ChooseYourMoney Story.com.**

ABOUT THE AUTHOR

JUNKO HORVATH is a CEO of Fujiyama Wealth Management in Atlanta, Georgia. She is a CERTIFIED FINANCIAL PLANNER™ and Certified Financial Transitionist® (CeFT®). With over 20 years of experience, she helps clients through Life Transitions, which are monumental events in one's life that  may require a financial expert—such as suddenly becoming single by the death of a spouse, transitioning through a divorce, receiving an inheritance, moving from the work force into retirement, selling a business, or winning the lottery. She is a seven-time recipient of the Five Star Wealth Manager Award which is given to the top 3% of financial advisors in Atlanta. In 2014 and 2015, she received the Women's Choice Award by the WIFE organization as one of the Top 100 Financial Advisors in the U.S. She has been featured in *Forbes*, *Fortune*, *WSJ*, *USA Today*, *Atlanta Magazine*, *Atlanta Jewish Times*, *Global Atlanta*, *Business RadioX*, and *Georgia Trend*.

Junko grew up in a traditional Japanese family where her father was a rainmaker and her mother was a homemaker. Her father managed the entire household's financials and her mother didn't know anything about money except the allowance she received from her husband monthly. Her mother's lack of financial independence made Junko determined to be a completely independent woman. After Junko moved to the US, and became a financial advisor, she assumed that her mother's situation was because of her heritage. However, she was shocked when she quickly realized that many American women, who were educated and had the ability to make choices, also felt stuck like her mother. They too lacked financial confidence, because they let their spouses handle all the financial decisions.

Discovering that this is a situation many women find themselves in regardless of age or culture made her decide that her mission as a financial advisor is to encourage every woman to be more engaged in their household finances. Junko's goal is to be their biggest cheerleader and to work alongside of them, giving them the support and knowledge them need, to confidently have a voice in how to manage their household finances.

She is a proud member of Balser Giving Circle to help unprivileged children and young adults. She has also raised money for a local school by conducting charity concerts by singing and introducing Japanese music and dance to the community. She served on many boards in the past including, Midtown Rotary Club, Grady Health System's Visiting Board, Torah Day School of Atlanta, Congregation Ariel, and Jewish Fertility Foundation. She lives in Atlanta with her husband, Stephen and her mother whom she brought over from Japan six years ago with her father who rests in peace in heaven. She has two married daughters, Yael and Adina & their families in Philadelphia, PA and Silver Spring, MD.

She welcomes your feedback. You can email junko@fuji yamawealth.com or reach her at (678) 736-5194.

A FREE GIFT FOR YOU!

I want you to be able to craft your new money story and leave behind the story which might have been created since you were a child.

This free gift will help you take a look at where you came from and where you are going and how to choose your new money story and destination.

Visit **www.ChooseYourMoneyStory.com** and download the gift today!

CHAPTER 1: DIVORCE

Andy Flink
Founder
Flink Family Law Mediation/Arbitration
www.andyflink.com

Randall D. Grayson, Attorney at Law
Partner
DelCampo & Grayson LLC
https://www.dcglawfirm.com/

Sherri S. Holder, CPA/ABV/CFF, CVA
Partner
The Holder Group, LLC
http://www.thgcpa.net/

Linda Klein
Former President of the American Bar Association, the first
woman President of the State Bar of Georgia, and Senior
Managing Shareholder at the Baker Donelson law firm
www.bakerdonelson.com

Alyson Lembeck
Family Law Attorney and Partner
Ellis Funk, P.C.
http://www.ellisfunk.com/

Emily W. McBurney, Esq.
QDRO Attorney
Emily W. McBurney, PC
http://www.emilyqdro.com/

Tracy Ann Moore-Grant
Founder of Amicable Divorce Network, Attorney, Mediator,
and Arbitrator, Patterson Moore Butler
https://amicabledivorcenetwork.com/
https://www.pattersonmoorebutler.com/

Tina Shadix Roddenbery
Family Law Attorney and Shareholder
Boyd, Collar, Nolen, Tuggle, & Roddenbery, LLC
https://www.bcntrlaw.com/

Catherine Sanderson
Family Law Attorney and Partner
Sanderson & Sanford, LLC
http://www.sandersonlaw.com/

Erin S. Stone
Family Law Attorney and Partner
Bovis, Kyle, Burch & Medlin, LLC
http://www.boviskyle.com/

Rob Tamburri, CPA
Managing Partner
Balog & Tamburri, CPAs
https://flgacpa.com/

Deborah Wilder, PhD
Psychologist, Divorce Mediator, Divorce Counselor, and
Parenting Coordinator

Center For Therapy and Mediation
https://www.drdeborahwilder.com/

CHAPTER 2: INHERITANCE

Donald B. DeLoach
Estate Planning Attorney
Caldwell, Propst & DeLoach, LLP
http://cpdlawyers.com/

Laurie Dyke, CPA
Managing Partner
IAG Forensics & Valuation
https://www.iagforensics.com/

David Golden
Estate and Tax Attorney and Partner
Troutman Pepper Hamilton Sanders LLP
https://www.troutman.com/

Linda Klein
Senior Managing Shareholder
Baker Donelson law firm
www.bakerdonelson.com

CHAPTER 3: RETIREMENT

Susan Brown
Senior Market Specialist
Multiplied Benefits Architecture, LLC
https://mba.agency/

Erica Dumpel
Medicare Counselor
Founder
Czajkowski, Dumpel & Associates, Inc.
http://cdainc.net/

Jonathan Ginsberg
Social Security Disability Attorney
Owner
Ginsberg Law Offices
https://glolaw.com

Heather K. Karrh
Partner
Rogers, Hofrichter, & Karrh, LLC
https://www.roholaw.com/

Linda Klein
Senior Managing Shareholder
Baker Donelson law firm
www.bakerdonelson.com

Rhoda Margolis, LCSW
Atlanta Chapter Co-Founder
The Transition Network
https://www.thetransitionnetwork.org/chapters-atlanta/
www.thetransitionnetwork.org

Joanne Y. Max, Ph.D.
Clinical Psychologist
Clinical Neuropsychologist
College Planning and Consulting
www.drjoannemax.com

Heather Schreiber, RICP®
Founder and President
HLS Retirement Consulting, LLC
https://www.hlsretirementconsulting.com/

CHAPTER 4: WIDOWHOOD

Patricia F. Ammari
Elder & Special Needs Law Attorney
The Ammari Firm, LLC
https://elderlawatlanta.com/

Ronnie Genser
President
Bereavement Navigators
https://bereavementnavigators.com/

Laura Jalbert, LCSW
Licensed Clinical Social Worker
Owner and Clinical Director
Mindful Transitions
https://www.mindfultransitions.com

Ira M. Leff
Elder Law Attorney
Ira M. Leff Attorney at Law
http://www.iraleff.com/

CHAPTER 5: SALE OF BUSINESS

Don H. Bravaldo, III
President
Bravaldo Capital Advisors
https://bravaldocapitaladvisors.com/

Denis Brown
Partner
PACE Capital Advisors
http://www.pacecapitaladvisors.com/

Sara Burden
President
Walden Businesses Inc.
https://waldenbus.com/

Jayden Doye, CPA
President
Prestige Accounting Solutions
https://accounting-atlanta.com/

Nancy Gault, CPA
Partner
Nichols, Cauley & Associates, LLC
https://nicholscauley.com/

Dan Jourdan
VP of National Sales and Business Development
The Oxford Highland Group
https://toxhg.com/

Mark D. Oldenburg
Corporate Law Attorney and Partner
Oldenburg & Stiner, P.C.
https://oldenburgstiner.com/

M. Everett "Rett" Peaden
Partner
Smith, Gambrell & Russell, LLP
https://www.sgrlaw.com

Neeli Shah
Estate and Business Succession Planning Attorney
The Law Offices of Neeli Shah, LLC
https://www.neelishahlaw.com/

Eric Togneri
Managing Director
Neri Capital Partners
http://www.nericap.com/

I would like to thank the women/men who contributed their stories in this book. Without your opening your heart and shared your life's stories, this book couldn't have been born. Thank you to:

Amanda Bunder (Chapter 1: Divorce)
Kosher Coordinator
Berman Commons Assisted Living

Amy Szumstein (Chapter 1: Divorce)
Health & Wellness Expert
Holistic Healing
http://holistichealingwithamy.com

Rabbi Binyomin Friedman (Chapter 1: Divorce)
Rabbi at Congregation Ariel
www.congariel.org

Taka (Chapter 1: Divorce)
Homemaker

Darren (Chapter 2: Inheritance)
(Anonymous)

Helen Scherrer-Diamond (Chapter 2: Inheritance)
Community Outreach Director for 2 Funeral homes
GA Licensed Insurance Agent in Accident & Sickness
and Life

Annette Tirabasso (Chapter 3: Retirement)
Retired Partner
Deloitte Consulting

Alan Smirin (Chapter 3: Retirement)
Ex-Owner, Tower East, Beer, Wine and Spirits
Realtor, Keller Williams

Cindy Lynch (Chapter 4: Widowhood)
Principal, Six20 Partners
http://six20partners.com/

Helen Hersch (Chapter 4: Widowhood)
Ex-Owner, Hersch's Supermarket

Jamie (Chapter 4: Widowhood)
(Anonymous)

Sarah (Chapter 4: Widowhood)

Jan Evans (Chapter 5: Sale of Business)
Ex-Owner
LaGrange Landscape

Roberta Scher (Chapter 5: Sale of Business)
Co-Founder, Paper Parlour
Co-Founder, Executive Editor KosherEye.com

And now you get various expert advices that you can apply today to your own situation. Written by Certified Financial Planner and Certified Financial Transitionist, this easy to read book is packed with practical advices that you can apply today.